Mastering Chinese Words

Expanding Your Vocabulary with 2500 of the Most Common Chinese Words

©Copyright 2020

All Rights Reserved. No part of this book may be reproduced in any form without permission in writing from the author. Reviewers may quote brief passages in reviews.

Disclaimer: No part of this publication may be reproduced or transmitted in any form or by any means, mechanical or electronic, including photocopying or recording, or by any information storage and retrieval system, or transmitted by email without permission in writing from the publisher.

While all attempts have been made to verify the information provided in this publication, neither the author nor the publisher assumes any responsibility for errors, omissions or contrary interpretations of the subject matter herein.

This book is for entertainment purposes only. The views expressed are those of the author alone, and should not be taken as expert instruction or commands. The reader is responsible for his or her own actions.

Adherence to all applicable laws and regulations, including international, federal, state and local laws governing professional licensing, business practices, advertising and all other aspects of doing business in the US, Canada, UK or any other jurisdiction is the sole responsibility of the purchaser or reader.

Neither the author nor the publisher assumes any responsibility or liability whatsoever on the behalf of the purchaser or reader of these materials. Any perceived slight of any individual or organization is purely unintentional.

Contents

INTRODUCTION 1
PART I..3
1,200 BASIC WORDS 3
CHAPTER 1. NOUNS 4
CHAPTER 2. VERBS AND AUXILIARY VERBS 24
CHAPTER 3. PRONOUNS AND ADJECTIVES 45
CHAPTER 4. NUMERALS AND MEASURE WORDS 55
CHAPTER 5. ADVERBS, PREPOSITIONS, AND CONJUNCTIONS............58
PART II 64
LEARN 1,300 OTHER WORDS 64
CHAPTER 6. NOUNS (A ~ Q)...65
CHAPTER 7 NOUNS (R ~ Z) 79
CHAPTER 8. VERBS (A ~ L) 90
CHAPTER 9 VERBS (M ~ Z) 104
CHAPTER 10. OTHER CONTENT AND FUNCTION WORDS (A ~ L)....118
CONCLUSION 136

Introduction

Within China, there are 56 nationalities, so you might be wondering what exactly is "Chinese language"? Well, it is "Han language".

In China, the Han population is the largest. The other 55 nationalities are referred to as minorities. As most people use the Han language, it has become the main tool for communication between the different nationalities.

The Chinese language has its own pronunciation and characters. Even though the Chinese people use the same characters, they may differ in their pronunciation from place to place because of the sheer size of the country. As a result, many dialects exist within China, e.g., Shanghai dialect, Guangdong dialect (Cantonese), etc. If a person from Shanghai uses the Shanghai dialect in Guangdong, few people would understand what is being said. This would also apply to people speaking Cantonese in Shanghai. Different dialects can make communication very difficult.

After the foundation of the People's Republic of China in 1949, the government made great efforts to spread Putonghua (Mandarin), the common language. Putonghua is now called "Modern Chinese". Pronunciation of Putonghua is based on the Beijing dialect, and the vocabulary is based on the north Chinese language. Now, Chinese people mainly use Putonghua to communicate. The Chinese language that you will learn in this book is Putonghua.

Learning Chinese characters is difficult, and because of this, people often lack the motivation to continue learning. In fact, to learn Chinese, it is not essential to learn the characters. To communicate verbally is often the learner's desire. Based on this, this book was created to expand your vocabulary. Usually, Chinese textbooks rely on learners to learn the characters. But here, Pinyin is introduced, allowing learners quickly to remember every word.

Now it is time to commence your lessons and learn the fascinating language of the Chinese.

Good luck!

PART I

1,200 BASIC WORDS

A word is the smallest meaningful unit in a language. Words are used as basic building blocks to express ideas. In this chapter, you will learn 1,200 basic words.

Chinese words represented by a single syllable are called monosyllabic words. Words represented by two syllables are called dissyllabic words. Words composed of three or more syllables are called polysyllabic words. In writing, a syllable is a character. As such, monosyllabic words are represented by one character, dissyllabic words by two, and polysyllabic words by more than two.

Chinese words can be divided into two kinds: notional and function words. Nouns, verbs, auxiliary verbs, adjectives, numerals, measure words, and pronouns belong to the notional word category. Adverbs, prepositions, conjunctions, particles, interjections, and onomatopes belong to the function word category.

Normally, a word belongs to a certain part of speech. Some words, however, have the grammatical function of two or more parts of speech. Remember to pay more attention to these words.

You shall deal with each part of speech separately.

Chapter 1. Nouns

In Chinese, the same form of a noun is used in the subject and object position. Except for the written form of third-person pronouns, Chinese nouns are not gendered, and there is no distinction between masculine, feminine, and neuter found in many European languages.

1. 家/jiā/ - home
2. 学校/xué xiào/ - school
3. 饭馆/fàn guǎn/ - restaurant
4. 餐厅/cān tīng/ - dining room; dining hall; restaurant
5. 商店/shāng diàn/ - shop; store
6. 医院/yī yuàn/ - hospital
7. 火车站/huǒ chē zhàn/ - train station
8. 公司/gōng sī/ - company
9. 机场/jī chǎng/ - airport
10. 教室/jiāo shì/ - classroom
11. 房间/fáng jiān/ - room
12. 路/lù/ - road; path
13. 超市/chāo shì/ - supermarket
14. 入口/rù kǒu/ - entrance
15. 公园/gōng yuán/ - park

16. 花园/huā yuán/ - garden
17. 图书馆/tú shū guǎn/ - library
18. 办公室/bàn gōng shì/ - office
19. 厨房/chú fáng/ - kitchen
20. 洗手间/xǐ shǒu jiān/ - washroom; toilet; lavatory
21. 厕所/cè suǒ/ - toilet
22. 银行/yín háng/ - bank
23. 宾馆/bīn guǎn/ - hotel
24. 加油站/jiā yóu zhàn/ - gas station
25. 大使馆/dà shǐ guǎn/ - embassy
26. 市场/shì chǎng/ - market
27. 长城/cháng chéng/ - the Great Wall
28. 长江/cháng jiāng/ - the Yangtze River
29. 黄河/huáng hé/ - Yellow River
30. 地方/dì fāng/ - place; region
31. 街道/jiē dào/ - street
32. 农村/nóng cūn/ - countryside; village
33. 城市/chéng shì/ - city
34. 北京/běi jīng/ - Beijing
35. 首都/shǒu dōu/ - capital
36. 省/shěng/ - province; to save

我们得想一种省钱的办法。- We have to think of a way to save money.

37. 中国/zhōng guó/ - China
38. 国家/guó jiā/ - country
39. 亚洲/yà zhōu/ - Asia
40. 世界/shì jiè/ - world
41. 地球/dì qiú/ - the Earth
42. 地点/dì diǎn/ - place; location
43. 上/shàng/ - up; on; last (week, etc.); Part I (of two parts)

书在桌子上。- The book is on the table.

我上周去了医院。- I went to the hospital last week.

《哈利·波特与死亡圣器·上》- Harry Potter and the Deathly Hallows Part I

44. 下/xià/ - down; under; below; next (week, month, year); Part II (of two parts)

他们在地下发现财宝。- They found treasure under the ground.

我下周要去北京。- I'm going to Beijing next week.

《哈利·波特与死亡圣器·下》- Harry Potter and the Deathly Hallows Part II

45. 前面/qián miàn/ - ahead; in front; preceding

46. 后面/hòu miàn/ - back; behind; afterward

47. 里/lǐ/ - inside; interior; Chinese mile (measure unit, 500 meters)

48. 左边/zuǒ biān/ - left side

49. 右边/yòu biān/ - right side

50. 外/wài/ - outside; external; foreign

51. 旁边/páng biān/ - side; to the side; beside

52. 中间/zhōng jiān/ - middle; between

我想要中间那个。- I want the middle one.

我不希望我们中间有秘密。- I don't want any secrets between us.

53. 附近/fù jìn/ - nearby; (in the) vicinity

54. 东/dōng/ - east

55. 西/xī/ - west

56. 南/nán/ - south

57. 北方/běi fāng/ - north; the northern part of a country

58. 周围/zhōu wéi/ - surroundings

59. 对面/duì miàn/ - opposite

60. 内/nèi/ - inside; internal

61. 底/dǐ/ - bottom; the end of (a period of time)

把洋葱片铺在盘底。- Spread the onion slices on the bottom of the dish.

我月底还你钱。- I'll pay you back at the end of this month.

62. 今天/jīn tiān/ - today

63. 明天/míng tiān/ - tomorrow

64. 昨天/zuó tiān/ - yesterday

65. 上午/shàng wǔ/ - morning

66. 中午/zhōng wǔ/ - noon; midday

67. 下午/xià wǔ/ - afternoon

68. 年/nián/ - year

69. 月/yuè/ - month; moon

70. 日/rì/ - day; sun

71. 星期/xīng qī/ - week

72. 点/diǎn/ - o'clock; dot; to order; to light (cigarette, fire, etc.)

八点了。- It is eight o'clock.
用绿点对它们进行了标记。- Mark them with a green dot.
她点了一份沙拉。- She ordered a salad.
如果我们抽烟的话，最好点一支让她也试试。- If we're going to smoke, we'd better light one and let her try it out as well.

73. 分钟/fēn zhōng/ - minute

74. 现在/xiàn zài/ - now; at present; at the moment

75. 时候/shí hòu/ - time; moment; period

你什么时候来？- What time will you be here?

76. 早上/zǎo shàng/ - morning

77. 晚上/wǎn shàng/ - evening; night

78. 小时/xiǎo shí/ - hour

79. 时间/shí jiān/ - time

80. 去年/qù nián/ - last year

81. 号/hào/ - day of month; (suffix used after) name of a ship; number

今天是二月二十号。- Today is February 20.

我最喜欢的电影是泰坦尼克号。- My favorite movie is *Titanic*.

你的房间号是606. - Your room number is 606.

82. 生日/shēng rì/ - birthday

83. 春/chūn/ - spring

84. 夏/xià/ - summer

85. 秋/qiū/ - autumn

86. 冬/dōng/ - winter

87. 季节/jì jié/ - season

88. 以前/yǐ qián/ - ago; previous; before; previous

89. 以后/yǐ hòu/ - later on

90. 过去/guò qù/ - (in the) past; previous; to pass by; to go over

91. 最近/zuì jìn/ - recently; lately; these days; nearest (of locations): shortest (of routes)

92. 周末/zhōu mò/ - weekend

93. 刚才/gāng cái/ - just now; a while ago

94. 将来/jiāng lái/ - future; in the future

95. 后来/hòu lái/ - afterward; later

96. 平时/píng shí/ - in normal times

97. 当时/dāng shí/ - at that time

98. 寒假/hán jiǎ/ - winter vacation

101. 人/rén/ - person; people; human

102. 男人/nán rén/ - man

103. 女人/nǚ rén/ - woman

104. 先生/xiān shēng/ - sir; Mr.

105. 小姐/xiǎo jiě/ - Miss; prostitute (slang)

106. 儿童/ér tóng/ - children

107. 爸爸/bà ba/ - dad; father

108. 父亲/fù qīn/ - father (written)
109. 妈妈/mā ma/ - mom; mother
110. 母亲/mǔ qīn/ - mother (written)
111. 儿子/ér zi/ - son
112. 女儿/nǚ ér/ - daughter
113. 爷爷/yé ye/ - grandfather (paternal)
114. 奶奶/nǎi nai/ - grandmother (paternal)
115. 孙子/sūn zi/ - grandson
116. 叔叔/shū shu/ - uncle; paternal younger brother
117. 阿姨/ā yí/ - aunt
118. 哥哥/gē ge/ - older brother
119. 姐姐/jiě jie/ - older sister
120. 弟弟/dì di/ - younger brother
121. 妹妹/mèi mei/ - younger sister
122. 丈夫/zhàng fu/ - husband
123. 妻子/qī zǐ/ - wife
124. 孩子/hái zi/ - child; kid
125. 亲戚/qīn qi/ - relative; kinsfolk
126. 老师/lǎo shī/ - teacher
127. 学生/xué shēng/ - student
128. 同学/tóng xué/ - classmate
129. 朋友/péng yǒu/ - friend
130. 医生/yī shēng/ - doctor
131. 服务员/fú wù yuán/ - waiter; waitress
132. 同事/tóng shì/ - colleague; coworker
133. 校长/xiào zhǎng/ - headmaster
134. 经理/jīng lǐ/ - manager
135. 司机/sī jī/ - driver
136. 邻居/lín jū/ - neighbor
137. 房东/fáng dǒng/ - landlord

138. 客人/kè rén/ - guest; customer
139. 师傅/shī fu/ - master
140. 演员/yǎn yuán/ - actor; actress
141. 警察/jǐng chá/ - police officer
142. 记者/jì zhě/ - journalist
143. 大夫/dài fu/ - doctor
144. 护士/hù shì/ - nurse
145. 顾客/gù kè/ - client; customer
146. 观众/guān zhòng/ - audience
147. 作者/zuò zhě/ - writer
148. 作家/zuò jiā/ - author
149. 教授/jiāo shòu/ - professor

委员会由教授和工程师组成。- The committee was composed of professors and engineers.

/jiāo shòu/ - to instruct; to teach

他们将教授阅读、写作和语法基础知识。- They will teach the basics of reading, writing, and grammar.

150. 研究生/yán jiū shēng/ - graduate student
151. 硕士/shuò shì/ - master's degree
152. 博士/bó shì/ - doctor; Ph.D.
153. 律师/lǜ shī/ - lawyer
154. 导游/dǎo yóu/ - tour guide
155. 售货员/shòu huò yuán/ - salesclerk; shop assistant
156. 衣服/yī fu/ - clothes
157. 衬衫/chèn shān/ - shirt
158. 裤子/kù zi/ - pants
159. 裙子/qún zi/ - skirt
160. 帽子/mào zi/ - hat; cap
161. 鞋/xié/ - shoes
162. 皮鞋/pí xié/ - leather shoes

163. 袜子/wà zi/ - socks
164. 眼镜/yǎn jìng/ - glasses
165. 饮料/yǐn liào/ - beverage; drink
166. 水/shuǐ/ - water
167. 茶/chá/ - tea
168. 啤酒/pí jiǔ/ - beer
169. 果汁/guǒ zhī/ - juice
170. 咖啡/kā fēi/ - coffee
171. 汤/tāng/ - soup
172. 食品/shí pǐn/ - food
173. 水果/shuǐ guǒ/ - fruit
174. 苹果/píng guǒ/ - apple
175. 西红柿/xī hóng shì/ - tomato
176. 香蕉/xiāng jiāo/ - banana
177. 葡萄/pú táo/ - grape
178. 西瓜/xī guā/ - watermelon
179. 菜/cài/ - vegetable; dish (type of food)
我不喜欢吃菜。- I don't like eating vegetables.
今晚上有几道菜？- How many dishes will be served tonight?
180. 米饭/mǐ fàn/ - (cooked) rice
181. 米/mǐ/ - rice; meter
182. 面条/miàn tiáo/ - noodles
183. 面包/miàn bāo/ - bread
184. 包子/bāo zi/ - steamed stuffed bun
185. 蛋糕/dàn gāo/ - cake
186. 糖/táng/ - sugar; sweet
187. 羊肉/yáng ròu/ - mutton
188. 牛奶/niú nǎi/ - milk
189. 鸡蛋/jī dàn/ - chicken egg
190. 饺子/jiǎo zi/ - dumpling

191. 盐/yán/ - salt
192. 巧克力/qiǎo kè lì/ - chocolate
193. 饼干/bǐng gàn/ - biscuit; cracker
194. 药/yào/ - pill; medicine
195. 植物/zhí wù/ - plant
196. 叶子/yè zi/ - leaf
197. 身体/shēn tǐ/ - body
198. 眼睛/yǎn jīng/ - eye
199. 头发/tóu fā/ - hair (on the head)
200. 脸/liǎn/ - face
201. 耳朵/ěr duo/ - ear
202. 口/kǒu/ - mouth; measure word for wells, woks, etc.
203. 嘴/zuǐ/ - mouth; beak; spout (of teapot, etc.)
204. 腿/tuǐ/ - leg
205. 胳膊/gē bo/ - arm
206. 脚/jiǎo/ - foot
207. 肚子/dù zi/ - belly
208. 鼻子/bí zi/ - nose
209. 皮肤/pí fū/ - skin
210. 血/xuè; xiě/ - blood
211. 汗/hàn/ - sweat
212. 动物/dòng wù/ - animal
213. 熊猫/xióng māo/ - panda
214. 鸟/niǎo/ - bird
215. 马/mǎ/ - horse
216. 老虎/lǎo hǔ/ - tiger
217. 猴子/hóu zi/ - monkey
218. 猪/zhū/ - pig
219. 狮子/shī zi/ - lion
220. 鱼/yú/ - fish

221. 猫/māo/ - cat

222. 狗/gǒu/ - dog

223. 河/hé/ - river

224. 树/shù/ - tree

225. 草/cǎo/ - grass; draft (of a document)

在写报告前我喜欢先打草。- Before writing a report, I like to make a draft.

226. 云/yún/ - cloud

227. 天气/tiān qì/ - weather

228. 雪/xuě/ - snow

229. 太阳/tài yáng/ - sun

230. 月亮/yuè liàng/ - moon

231. 空气/kōng qì/ - air

232. 阳光/yáng guāng/ - sunshine; sunlight

233. 海洋/hǎi yáng/ - sea; ocean

234. 火/huǒ/ - fire; to be popular; to be furious

这屋里有火。- There is fire in this room.

这部电影非常火。- This movie is very popular.

听到有人背后说他坏话，他火了。- After hearing someone speak ill of him behind his back, he became furious.

235. 森林/sēn lín/ - forest

236. 桥/qiáo/ - bridge

237. 公共汽车/gōng gòng qì chē/ - bus

238. 船/chuán/ - boat; ship; vessel

239. 飞机/fēi jī/ - plane

240. 航班/háng bān/ - flight

241. 出租车/chū zū chē/ - taxi; cab

242. 自行车/zì xíng chē/ - bike; bicycle

243. 地铁/dì tiě/ - subway; underground train

244. 座位/zuò wèi/ - seat

245. 电梯/diàn tī/ - elevator; lift; escalator

246. 楼/lóu/ - building; floor

这是一座写字楼。- This is an office building.

他住在三楼。- He lives on the third floor.

247. 地址/dì zhǐ/ - address

248. 墙/qiáng/ - wall

249. 窗户/chuāng hù/ - window

250. 门/mén/ - door; measure word (for courses, subjects, etc.); Phylum (biology)

开门！- Open the door!

我们这学期有两门新课。- We have two new courses in this semester.

251. 东西/dōng xi/ - thing; direction; person (when talking about someone angrily)

这是什么东西？- What is this thing?

她一出门就东西不分。- As soon as she goes out, she can't tell the direction.

他真不是东西！- He's not a person! (He's a nut!)

252. 家具/jiā jù/ - furniture

253. 桌子/zhuō zi/ - table; desk

254. 椅子/yǐ zi/ - chair

255. 杯子/bēi zi/ - cup; mug

256. 电视/diàn shì/ - television

257. 电脑/diàn nǎo/ - computer

258. 手机/shǒu jī/ - mobile phone

259. 手表/shǒu biǎo/ - watch

260. 报纸/bào zhǐ/ - newspaper

261. 冰箱/bīng xiāng/ - fridge; refrigerator

262. 灯/dēng/ - light; lamp; lantern

263. 伞/sǎn/ - umbrella

264. 盘子/pán zi/ - plate; tray

265. 碗/wǎn/ - bowl

266. 筷子/kuài zi/ - chopsticks

267. 铅笔/qiān bǐ/ - pencil

268. 地图/dì tú/ - map

269. 礼物/lǐ wù/ - gift; present

270. 包/bāo/ - bag; kit; to wrap; to take charge of; to cover; Bao (surname); measure word (for things packed in a bag)

翻包侵犯隐私。- A bag search is an invasion of privacy.

你能帮我把它包起来吗？- Could you help me wrap this?

这件事包在我身上。- I'll take care of this. (Consider it done.)

费用公司包了。- The company will cover the costs.

一包零食 - A bag of snacks

急救包 - First-aid kit

271. 行李箱/xíng lǐ xiāng/ - suitcase

272. 信/xìn/ - letter

273. 书/shū/ - book

274. 照片/zhào piàn/ - photo

275. 照相机/zhào xiàng jī/ - camera

276. 空调/kōng tiáo/ - air conditioner

277. 菜单/cài dān/ - menu

278. 洗衣机/xǐ yī jī/ - washing machine

279. 沙发/shā fā/ - sofa; couch

280. 毛巾/máo jīn/ - towel

281. 牙膏/yá gāo/ - toothpaste

282. 工具/gōng jù/ - tool

283. 刀/dāo/ - knife

284. 镜子/jìng zi/ - mirror

285. 瓶子/píng zi/ - bottle

286. 盒子/hé zi/ - box

287. 塑料袋/sù liào dài/ - plastic bag
288. 钥匙/yào shi/ - key
289. 垃圾桶/lā jī tǒng/ - trash can; dustbin
290. 乒乓球/pīng pāng qiú/ - table tennis; ping pong
291. 羽毛球/yǔ máo qiú/ - badminton
292. 网球/wǎng qiú/ - tennis
293. 信用卡/xìn yòng kǎ/ - credit card
294. 钱/qián/ - money
295. 人民币/rén mín bì/ - RMB; Chinese yuan
296. 票/piào/ - ticket
297. 登机牌/dēng jī pái/ - boarding pass
298. 黑板/hēi bǎn/ - blackboard
299. 电子邮件/diàn zǐ yóu jiàn/ - email
300. 护照/hù zhào/ - passport
301. 签证/qiān zhèng/ - visa
302. 表格/biǎo gé/ - chart; spreadsheet; form
303. 杂志/zá zhì/ - magazine
304. 字典/zì diǎn/ - dictionary
305. 词典/cí diǎn/ - dictionary
306. 笔记本/bǐ jì běn/ - notebook
307. 日记/rì jì/ - diary; journal
308. 文章/wén zhāng/ - article; essay
309. 短信/duǎn xìn/ - text message
310. 报道/bào dào/ - report
311. 名字/míng zì/ - name
312. 汉语/hàn yǔ/ - Chinese (language)
313. 字/zì/ - word; character
314. 题/tí/ - exam question; to inscribe
315. 课/kè/ - class; course
316. 姓/xìng/ - surname

317. 问题/wèn tí/ - question

318. 错误/cuò wù/ - mistake; error

319. 事情/shì qing/ - matter

320. 考试/kǎo shì/ - exam; quiz

321. 意思/yì si/ - meaning

322. 颜色/yán sè/ - color

323. 味道/wèi dào/ - flavor; smell

324. 环境/huán jìng/ - environment; circumstance

325. 句子/jù zi/ - sentence

326. 词语/cí yǔ/ - vocabulary

327. 年级/nián jí/ - grade (at school)

328. 班/bān/ - work shift; class; surname Ban

329. 练习/liàn xí/ - practice; to practice

330. 作业/zuò yè/ - homework; to work

老师布置了很多作业。- The teacher assigned a lot of homework.

工地上有很多挖掘机正在作业。- There are many excavators working on the construction site.

331. 历史/lì shǐ/ - history

332. 数学/shù xué/ - math

333. 体育/tǐ yù/ - physical education

334. 音乐/yīn yuè/ - music

335. 爱好/ài hào/ - hobby

336. 比赛/bǐ sài/ - match; race; contest; competition

337. 节目/jié mù/ - show

我喜欢没有主持人的综艺节目。- I prefer variety shows without hosts.

338. 演出/yǎn chū/ - to act (in a play); to put on (a performance); to perform.

339. 节/jié/ - festival; measure word for segments (lessons, wagons, batteries, etc.)

340. 机会/jī huì/ - opportunity; chance

341. 文化/wén huà/ - culture

342. 习惯/xí guàn/ - habit; to get used to
他有很多不好的习惯。- He has many bad habits.
她习惯天天早起。- She is used to getting up early.

343. 新闻/xīn wén/ - news

344. 电影/diàn yǐng/ - movie

345. 小说/xiǎo shuō/ - novel

346. 京剧/jīng jù/ - Beijing Opera

347. 故事/gù shì/ - story

348. 游戏/yóu xì/ - game

349. 兴趣/xìng qù/ - interest

350. 功夫/gōng fu/ - Kung Fu; time; effort
来一趟费不了你多少功夫。- It won't take you much time to get here.
做这件事毫不费功夫。- It doesn't take much effort to do it.

351. 声音/shēng yīn/ - sound; voice

352. 水平/shuǐ píng/ - level (of achievement, etc.); horizontal

353. 关系/guān xi/ - relationship; relation

354. 办法/bàn fǎ/ - means; method

355. 作用/zuò yòng/ - function; effect; to act on
这种药有什么作用？- What effects does this medicine have?
摩擦力作用于运动着的物体，并使其停止。- Friction acts on moving objects and brings them to a stop.

356. 成绩/chéng jì/ - achievement; performance records; grades

357. 普通话/pǔ tōng huà/ - Mandarin

358. 会议/huì yì/ - meeting; conference

359. 性别/xìng bié/ - gender; sex

360. 年龄/nián líng/ - (a person's) age

361. 号码/hào mǎ/ - number
你的房间号码是多少？- What's your room number?

362. 数字/shù zì/ - number; figure; digit

363. 气候/qì hòu/ - climate

364. 答案/dá àn/ - answer

365. 广告/guǎng gào/ - advertisement

366. 传真/chuán zhēn/ - fax

367. 自然/zì rán/ - nature; natural; naturally

368. 风景/fēng jǐng/ - scenery

369. 材料/cái liào/ - material

370. 价格/jià gé/ - price

371. 奖金/jiǎng jīn/ - bonus

372. 工资/gōng zī/ - wage; salary

373. 堵车/dǔ chē/ - traffic jam

374. 收入/shōu rù/ - income

375. 部分/bù fen/ - part; section
中国是世界的一部分。- China is a part of the world.
本堂课的第一部分是听力练习。- The first section of this class is to practice your listening skills.

376. 距离/jù lí/ - distance

377. 数量/shù liàng/ - quantity; amount

378. 速度/sù dù/ - speed

379. 方向/fāng xiàng/ - direction

380. 质量/zhì liàng/ - quality

381. 温度/wēn dù/ - temperature

382. 过程/guò chéng/ - process

383. 顺序/shùn xù/ - order

384. 特点/tè diǎn/ - feature; characteristic

385. 效果/xiào guǒ/ - effect

386. 结果/jié guǒ/ - result
387. 目的/mù de/ - target; goal; purpose
388. 关键/guān jiàn/ - key; crucial
这是解决问题的关键。- This is the key to solving the problem.
目前危机正进入决定性的关键阶段。- The crisis is now entering a crucial critical phase.
389. 压力/yā lì/ - pressure
390. 心情/xīn qíng/ - mood
391. 脾气/pí qì/ - temper
392. 动作/dòng zuò/ - action; movement
393. 个子/gè zi/ - (in reference to) one's height or size
他是个大个子。- He's a big guy. (He's a tall guy.)
他个子高。- He's a tall guy.
他是个小个子。- He's a small guy. (He's a short guy.)
他个子矮。- He's a short guy.
394. 好处/hǎo chù/ - benefit
这么做有什么好处？- What are the benefits of doing so?
395. 优点/yōu diǎn/ - advantage
396. 缺点/quē diǎn/ - disadvantage
397. 基础/jī chǔ/ - base; foundation; basis
398. 重点/zhòng diǎn/ - focal point
399. 方法/fāng fǎ/ - method; way
400. 精神/jīng shén/ - spirit; mind (of a person)
401. 感情/gǎn qíng/ - emotion; feeling; relationship
感情不能代替政策。- Emotion should never be a substitute for sound policy.
别伤他的感情。- Don't hurt his feelings.
我们感情很好。- We have a good relationship.
402. 感觉/gǎn jué/ - feeling; to feel; to think
这给了我一种满足的感觉。- It gave me a feeling of satisfaction.

这一幕让你有什么感觉？ - How does this make you feel?

我感觉应该这么做。 - I think we need to do like this.

403. 印象/yìn xiàng/ - impression

404. 职业/zhí yè/ - occupation; professional

405. 专业/zhuān yè/ - major (at university); specialization; profession

406. 信心/xìn xīn/ - confidence; faith

407. 主意/zhǔ yì/ - idea; plan

408. 理想/lǐ xiǎng/ - ideal; perfection; perfect

409. 样子/yàng zi/ - looks

410. 力气/lì qì/ - strength

411. 态度/tài dù/ - attitude

412. 礼貌/lǐ mào/ - courtesy

413. 能力/néng lì/ - capability; ability

414. 经验/jīng yàn/ - experience

415. 任务/rèn wù/ - mission; assignment; task

416. 技术/jì shù/ - technology; skill

417. 责任/zé rèn/ - responsibility; duty

418. 性格/xìng gé/ - personality; character

419. 条件/tiáo jiàn/ - condition

420. 看法/kàn fǎ/ - viewpoint; opinion; way of looking at a thing

421. 困难/kùn nán/ - difficulty; difficult

422. 交通/jiāo tōng/ - transportation

423. 经济/jīng jì/ - economy; economic

424. 社会/shè huì/ - society

425. 国际/guó jì/ - international

426. 国籍/guó jí/ - nationality

427. 法律/fǎ lǜ/ - law

428. 艺术/yì shù/ - art

429. 科学/kē xué/ - science; scientific

430. 知识/zhī shi/ - knowledge

431. 内容/nèi róng/ - content

432. 语言/yǔ yán/ - language

433. 中文/zhōng wén/ - Chinese (language)

434. 语法/yǔ fǎ/ - grammar

435. 对话/duì huà/ - dialog

436. 方面/fāng miàn/ - aspect

437. 情况/qíng kuàng/ - circumstance; situation

438. 原因/yuán yīn/ - cause; reason

439. 教育/jiào yù/ - education; to educate

450. 计划/jì huá/ - plan; to plan

451. 标准/biāo zhǔn/ - standard

452. 规定/guī dìng/ - regulation; rule; to stipulate

453. 活动/huó dòng/ - activity; to exercise; loose

你需要稍微多活动一下。- You need to exercise a bit more.

这个螺丝活动了。- This screw is loose.

454. 经历/jīng lì/ - experience; to experience

455. 实际/shí jì/ - reality; actual

456. 友谊/yǒu yì/ - friendship

457. 友情/yǒu qíng/ - friendship

458. 生活/shēng huó/ - life; to live

外国的生活方式与我们不同。- Foreign countries have a different way of life from us.

他靠正当的劳动生活。- He lives by honest labor.

459. 生命/shēng mìng/ - life

生命是怎么起源的？- How did life begin?

460. 生意/shēng yi/ - business

461. 民族/mín zú/ - ethnic group

462. 爱情/ài qíng/ - love

463. 世纪/shì jì/ - century

464. 消息/xiāo xī/ – news; information
465. 网站/wǎng zhàn/ – website
466. 互联网/hù lián wǎng/ – the internet
467. 梦/mèng/ – dream
468. 密码/mì mǎ/ – password
469. 区别/qū bié/ – difference; to distinguish
470. 笑话/xiào huà/ – joke
471. 范围/fàn wéi/ – scope

Chapter 2. Verbs and Auxiliary Verbs

Chinese verbs do not conjugate like verbs from most Indo-European languages, such as English or Spanish. In fact, there is no strict morphological change in the Chinese language. The form of a verb remains unchanged under all circumstances. Differences in person, gender, and instances do not require changes in the form of a verb.

472. 谢谢/xiè xie/ – to thank; thanks

473. 不客气/bú kè qi/ – you're welcome; it's my pleasure

474. 再见/zài jiàn/ – goodbye

475. 请/qǐng/ – please (do something); to treat (to a meal, etc.) 他要请我看球赛。– He's going to treat me to a football match.

476. 对不起/duì bù qǐ/ – I'm sorry; excuse me; pardon me

477. 没关系/méi guān xi/ – don't worry about it

478. 欢迎/huān yíng/ – to welcome

479. 是/shì/ – be (to express judgment, existence or denote classification)

480. 有/yǒu/ – to have; there be

481. 看/kàn/ – to look at
/kān/ – to guard

有两个入口的房子很难看守。- A house with two entrances is difficult to guard.

482. 听/tīng/ - to listen; to hear; to obey; measure word for canned beverages

483. 说话/shuō huà/ - to speak; to say

484. 读/dú/ - to read; to pronounce

485. 写/xiě/ - to write

486. 看见/kàn jiàn/ - to see

487. 叫/jiào/ - to call; to shout; to order
你叫我什么？- What did you call me?
别叫了！- Stop shouting!
我给你叫辆出租车吧。- Let me order a taxi for you.

488. 来/lái/ - to come; to arrive

489. 回/huí/ - to go back; to return; measure word (for acts of a play); section or chapter (of a classical book)

490. 去/qù/ - to go; to go to (a place); to remove; to delete
请把这一段去了。- Please delete this paragraph.

491. 吃/chī/ - to eat

492. 喝/hē/ - to drink

493. 睡觉/shuì jiào/ - to go to sleep; to go to bed

494. 打电话/dǎ diàn huà/ - to make a phone call

495. 做/zuò/ - to do; to make; to produce

496. 买/mǎi/ - to buy; to purchase

497. 卖/mài/ - to sell

498. 开/fān/ - to open; to start; to turn on; to operate (vehicle, ship, plane, etc.)

499. 坐/zuò/ - to sit; to take (a bus, airplane, etc.)

500. 住/zhù/ - to live; to dwell; to stay

501. 学习/xué xí/ - to learn; to study

502. 工作/gōng zuò/ - to work; job

他在工作。- He's working now.

他需要一份工作。- He needs a job.

503. 下雨/xià yǔ/ - rain

504. 问/wèn/ - to ask

505. 走/zǒu/ - to walk; to go; to leave

506. 进/jìn/ - to enter; to go into

507. 出/chū/ - to go out; to come out; measure word (for dramas, plays, operas, etc.)

508. 赶/gǎn/ - to catch up with; to try to catch (the bus, etc.); to drive (someone/something) away; to drive (cattle, etc.) forward

我赶不上他。- I couldn't catch up with him.

他要赶末班车。- He's trying to catch the last bus.

我被她从屋里赶出来了。- She drove me out of the house.

牧羊人把羊群向前赶。- The shepherd drove the sheep forward.

509. 跑步/pǎo bù/ - to run; to take a walk

510. 到/dào/ - to (a place); until (a time); to arrive; to go

511. 穿/chuān/ - to wear; to put on

512. 洗/xǐ/ - to wash

513. 给/gěi/ - to give; to do something (for someone); for (someone); (for an imperative tone)

你能把那个盒子给我吗？- Can you give me that box?

他给我带来了圣诞礼物。- He brought me a Christmas present.

这是给她的。- This is for her.

你给我过来！- Come here, now!

514. 找/zhǎo/ - to look for; to call on someone; to find; to give change

515. 付款/fù kuǎn/ - to pay

516. 懂/dǒng/ - to understand; to know

517. 笑/xiào/ - to laugh; to smile

518. 回答/huí dá/ - to reply; to answer; answer

519. 告诉/gào sù/ - to tell; to inform

520. 准备/zhǔn bèi/ - to prepare; preparation

521. 开始/kāi shǐ/ - to begin; to start; beginning

522. 介绍/jiè shào/ - to introduce

523. 帮助/bāng zhù/ - to help; to assist; help; assistance

524. 玩/wán/ - to play

525. 送/sòng/ - to give (as a present); to see off; to send

我送了她一条项链。- I gave her a necklace.

我得去送我父母。- I have to see off my parents.

请把这些样品送北京去。- Please send these samples to Beijing.

526. 等/děng/ - to wait for; and so on; as soon as, etc.

请等我一会儿。- Please wait for me for a while.

527. 我喜欢体育运动，如打篮球、踢足球等。- I like sports; for example, basketball, soccer, and so on.

等他来了我们就能开始。- We can get started as soon as he arrives.

528. 让/ràng/ - to let someone do something; to give something willingly

让她进来吧。- Let her in.

这件外套我让给你了。- I'll give you this coat.

529. 起床/qǐ chuáng/ - to get up

530. 唱歌/chàng gē/ - to sing a song

531. 跳舞/tiào wǔ/ - to dance

532. 旅游/lǚ yóu/ - to go on a trip; travel; tour

533. 旅行/lǚ xíng/ - to travel; journey; trip

534. 上班/shàng bān/ - to go to work

535. 生病/shēng bìng/ - to fall ill

536. 休息/xiū xi/ - to rest; rest

537. 运动/yùn dòng/ - to exercise; sports

538. 游泳/yóu yǒng/ - to swim; swimming

539. 踢足球/tī zú qiú/ - to play football

540. 打篮球/dǎ lán qiú/ - to play basketball

541. 完/wán/ - to finish; to be over

542. 差/chāi/ - to assign (someone to do something)

老板差我去买烟。- The boss told me to buy cigarettes.

/chā/ - bad (student); difference (math)

他是个差生。- He's a bad student.

/chà/ - bad; wrong; poor (quality); to lack

这件外套质量很差。- The quality of this coat is poor.

这道题你做差了。- You've done wrong on this question.

他态度很差。- He has a bad attitude.

她离终点就差那么一点儿。- She only a little bit from the finish line. (She's so close to the finish line.)

543. 刮风/guā fēng/ - to be windy

544. 建议/jiàn yì/ - to suggest; to recommend; suggestion; recommendation

545. 感冒/gǎn mào/ - to catch cold

546. 发烧/fā shāo/ - to have a fever

547. 生气/shēng qì/ - to get angry

548. 哭/kū/ - to cry; to weep

549. 满意/mǎn yì/ - to be satisfied; satisfaction

550. 忘记/wàng jì/ - to forget

551. 照顾/zhào gù/ - to take care of (someone); to look after; care

552. 画/huà/ - to draw; painting

553. 带/dài/ - to carry; to bring; to take; to lead

带上这个！- Take this!

带路吧！- Lead the way!

把他带来。- Bring him to me.

你不能带这个。- You can't carry this.

554. 放/fàng/ – to set off (fire, fireworks, etc.); to release; to let go; to put; to place

555. 讲/jiǎng/ – to speak

556. 用/yòng/ – to use

557. 存/cún/ – to save; to keep; to store

558. 借/jiè/ – to borrow

559. 还/huán/ – to return (money, books, etc.)
/hái/ – still; yet
你怎么还在这儿？– Why are you still here?
我还没走。– I haven't gone yet.

560. 把/bǎ/ – to hold; measure word for chairs and objects with handles
帮我把一下门。– Please hold the door for me.

561. 拿/ná/ – to hold; to take
拿着。– Hold this.
把它拿走吧。– Just take it away.

562. 站/zhàn/ – to stand; station

563. 像/xiàng/ – to look like; to be similar to; image; portrait

564. 接/jiē/ – to answer (the phone); to pick someone up
没人接我电话。– No one answered my phone.
谢谢你来机场接我。– Thank you for picking me up from the airport.

565. 转/zhuǎn/ – to turn; to change direction; to transfer; to forward (mail, phone call)
/zhuàn/ – to spin

566. 搬/bān/ – to move

567. 倒/dào/ – to move backward
/dǎo/ – to fall

568. 花/huā/ – to spend (money, time); blossom

569. 教/jiāo/ – to teach

570. 换/huàn/ – to change; to exchange

571. 关/guān/ - to close; to shut; to turn off; mountain pass

572. 骑/qí/ - to ride

573. 复习/fù xí/ - to revise; to review; revision

574. 发现/fā xiàn/ - to find

575. 打算/dǎ suàn/ - to plan; to intend; intention; plan

你打算做什么？- What do you intend to do?

你有什么打算？- What's your plan?

576. 决定/jué dìng/ - to decide; decision

577. 认为/rèn wéi/ - to believe; to think; to consider; to feel

578. 选择/xuǎn zé/ - to choose; to select; choice

579. 表演/biǎo yǎn/ - to act; to perform; show; performance

580. 同意/tóng yì/ - to agree; to approve

581. 明白/míng bái/ - to understand; to realize

582. 了解/le jiě/ - to understand; to realize; to find out

583. 举行/jǔ xíng/ - to hold (meetings, ceremony, etc.)

584. 举办/jǔ bàn/ - to hold (events, activities, etc.)

585. 变化/biàn huà/ - to change; change

586. 提高/tí gāo/ - to improve

587. 出现/chū xiàn/ - to appear; to show up

588. 检查/jiǎn chá/ - to inspect; to examine; inspection

589. 学习/xué xí/ - to study; study

590. 研究/yán jiū/ - to research; research

591. 遇到/yù dào/ - to run into; to come across

592. 解决/jiě jué/ - to solve

593. 迟到/chí dào/ - to be late

594. 影响/yǐng xiǎng/ - to influence; to disturb; influence; effect

他正在试图影响警察的判断。- He is trying to influence the judgment of the police.

别影响我！- Don't disturb me.

我当时深受一位历史老师的影响。- I was deeply influenced by a history teacher at the time.

595. 需要/xū yào/ - to need; to want; to demand; needs

596. 注意/zhù yì/ - to pay attention to; to focus; to notice;

597. 要求/yāo qiú/ - to ask; to demand; to request; to require; requirement

598. 离开/lí kāi/ - to leave

599. 爬山/pá shān/ - to climb a mountain; to go hiking

600. 锻炼/duàn liàn/ - to exercise; exercise

601. 洗澡/xǐ zǎo/ - to take a shower

602. 参加/cān jiā/ - to participate; to join

603. 见面/jiàn miàn/ - to meet; to see someone

604. 完成/wán chéng/ - to complete; to finish; to accomplish

605. 结束/jié shù/ - to finish; to end; termination

606. 结婚/jié hūn/ - to marry; to get married

607. 表示/biǎo shì/ - to express; to indicate; to show

608. 刷牙/shuā yá/ - to brush one's teeth

609. 上网/shàng wǎng/ - to be on the internet

610. 留学/liú xué/ - to study abroad

611. 根据/gēn jù/ - to be based on; according to; basis; foundation

612. 疼/téng/ - to love; ache; sore

奶奶很疼我。- My grandmother loves me.

我头疼。- I have a headache.

我背疼。- I have a sore back.

613. 以为/yǐ wéi/ - to think; to believe

614. 打扫/dǎ sǎo/ - to clean; to sweep

615. 干/gàn/ - to do (some work)

/gān/ - dry

616. 拉/lā/ - to pull; to drag

617. 抱/bào/ - to hug; to embrace

618. 推/tuī/ - to push forward

619. 扔/rēng/ - to throw (away)

620. 挂/guà/ - to hang (from a hook, etc.); to hang up (a phone call); to be killed (colloquial); to cheat (in the game)

他刚上战场就挂了。 - He was killed as soon as he went to war.

这个玩家开挂！ - This player is cheating!

621. 抬/tái/ - to raise; (of two or more persons) to carry

能帮我抬一下吗？ - Can you help me to carry this?

抬起头来。 - Raise your head.

622. 举/jǔ/ - to raise (something overhead)

举起手来！ - Raise your hands! (Hands up!)

623. 提/tí/ - to lift; to raise; to carry (in one's hand with the arm down); to mention

他提着一袋米。 - He was carrying a bag of rice.

别提了。 - Don't mention it.

624. 撞/zhuàng/ - to hit

625. 擦/cā/ - to wipe

626. 指/zhǐ/ - to point at; to point to; to indicate; to refer to

627. 戴/dài/ - to put on or wear (glasses, hat, gloves, etc.)

628. 尝/cháng/ - to taste

629. 躺/tǎng/ - to lie down

630. 敲/qiāo/ - to knock (at a door); to hit

631. 表扬/biǎo yáng/ - to praise; to commend

632. 道歉/dào qiàn/ - to apologize

633. 商量/shāng liàng/ - to talk over; to discuss

634. 抽烟/chōu yān/ - to smoke (a cigarette)

635. 咳嗽/ké sòu/ - to cough

636. 收拾/shōu shí/ - to tidy up; to give someone a lesson (colloquial)

我去收拾他！ - I'll teach him a lesson!

637. 握手/wò shǒu/ - to shake hands

638. 鼓掌/gǔ zhǎng/ - to applaud

639. 打针/dǎ zhēn/ - to have or gave an injection

640. 值得/zhí dé/ - to be worth; to deserve

641. 逛/guàng/ - to stroll; to walk around

642. 流泪/liú lèi/ - to weep

643. 起来/qǐ lái/ - to rise; to stand up; (beginning or continuing an action)
说着说着她就哭了起来。- While talking, she began to cry.
说着说着她又哭了起来。- While talking, she cried again.

644. 散步/sàn bù/ - to take a walk; to go for a walk

645. 死/sǐ/ - to die; to be dead

646. 赢/yíng/ - to win

647. 输/shū/ - to lose; to enter (a password)

648. 断/duàn/ - to break

649. 丢/diū/ - to lose; to throw
他钱包丢了。- He lost his wallet.
麻烦你把那个帽子丢过来。- Please throw that hat over.

650. 掉/diào/ - to fall; to lose; to turn
秋天，树叶纷纷从树上掉下来。- Leaves fall off the trees in the autumn.
他钱包掉了。- He lost his wallet.
此路不通，请掉头！- This road is blocked, please turn around!

651. 增加/zēng jiā/ - to raise; to increase

652. 增长/zēng zhǎng/ - to grow

653. 减少/jiǎn shǎo/ - to reduce; to decrease

654. 通过/tōng guò/ - to pass through; to get through; by means of
你不能从这儿通过。- You're not allowed to pass through here.
通过这件事，我认识到自己的不足。- I realized my shortcomings from this incident.

655. 进行/jìn xíng/ - to carry on; in progress
会议的准备工作正在进行。- Preparations for the meeting are in progress.
我希望能进行一段时间。- I hope to carry on for an indeterminate period.

656. 继续/jì xù/ - to continue

657. 成为/chéng wéi/ - to become; to turn into

658. 提前/tí qián/ - to advance; to bring forward; in advance

659. 降低/jiàng dī/ - to lower; to reduce; to bring down

660. 降落/jiàng luò/ - to land

661. 获得/huò dé/ - to obtain

662. 接受/jiē shòu/ - to accept

663. 拒绝/jù jué/ - to refuse; to decline; to reject

664. 取/qǔ/ - to take; to get; to fetch

665. 成功/chéng gōng/ - to succeed; success
他成功当上了厂长。- He succeeded in becoming the factory manager.
失败是成功之母。- Failure is the mother of success.

666. 失败/shī bài/ - to fail; to lose; to be defeated; failure

667. 陪/péi/ - to accompany

668. 剩/shèng/ - to be left; to remain

669. 当/dāng/ - to be; when; to (do something, say something to) one's face; at (a time or place); to take responsibility
我想当科学家。- I want to be a scientist.
当我无聊的时候，我喜欢听歌。- I like listening to music when I'm bored.
你在当着我的面撒谎。- You are telling me lies to my face.
你当时怎么做的？- What did you do at that time?
一人做事一人当。- One should take responsibility for their actions.

/dàng/ - to think; to pawn; that very (day, etc.); to treat as; to take for

我当是她呢。- I thought it was her.

他把表当了。- He pawned his watch.

他父亲突然病重，当月就过世了。- His father suddenly got seriously ill and died that month.

不要把我当小孩看。- Don't treat me like a child.

670. 寄/jì/ - to send; to mail

671. 修/xiū/ - to fix; to repair

672. 修理/xiū lǐ/ - to repair; to fix; to teach someone a lesson (colloquial)

673. 弄/nòng/ - to play with; to make someone do something; to do; to get someone or something into a specified condition; to get

别弄我的头发。- Don't play with my hair.

别把孩子弄哭了。- Don't make the child cry.

弄得不好，就会前功尽弃。- If we don't do a good job now, all the work we've done will be wasted.

他把衣服弄脏了。- He got his clothes dirty.

你去弄点水来。- Go and get some water.

674. 养成/yǎng chéng/ - to cultivate

675. 过/guò/ - to cross; to pass; to spend (time); after; to undergo a process; over; to exceed; past; to live; to celebrate; excessively; demerit

过街时注意车辆。- When crossing the street, watch out for cars.

假期过得怎么样？- How did you spend your holiday?

过了夏至，天就开始变短。- The days get shorter after the summer solstice.

我们再过一遍这篇稿子。- Let's go over the draft once again.

他已经年过70了。- He's over 70 years old.

小鹿跳过篱笆墙。- The deer jumped over a fence.

小心别坐过了站。- Be sure you don't go past your station.

她过得很开心。- She lives a happy life.

我们明天给他过生日。- We will celebrate his birthday tomorrow.

他已被记过三次。- He already has three demerits on his record.

这位经理还被指责给自己支付过高的薪水。- This manager is also accused of paying himself an excessively high salary.

676. 留/liú/ - to stay; to keep; to leave; to remain

677. 试/shì/ - to try; to test

678. 脱/tuō/ - to take off

679. 赚/zhuàn/ - to earn; to make a profit

680. 租/zū/ - to rent

681. 填空/tián kòng/ - to fill in a blank

682. 发/fā/ - to send out; measure word for gunshots

683. 骗/piàn/ - to cheat; to deceive; to fool

684. 猜/cāi/ - to guess

685. 发生/fā shēng/ - to happen; to take place; to occur

686. 引起/yǐn qǐ/ - to lead to; to cause

687. 使用/shǐ yòng/ - to use

688. 管理/guǎn lǐ/ - to manage; to supervise; management; administration

689. 批评/pī píng/ - to criticize; criticism

690. 适合/shì hé/ - to fit; to suit; suitable

绿色很适合你。- Green suits you.

我找不到适合的衣服。- I can't find clothes that fit me.

她没有其他适合这种场合穿的套裙。- She had no other dress suitable for the occasion.

691. 适应/shì yīng/ - to fit; to adapt; to get used to something

他过去从未干过这种工作，我不确定他能适应。- He's never done this type of work before; I'm not sure how he'll fit in.

这些样式可以修改，以适应个人不同爱好。- These styles can be adapted to suit individual tastes.

692. 吸引 /xī yǐn/ - to attract

693. 提供 /tí gōng/ - to provide; to offer

694. 交流 /jiāo liú/ - to communicate; communication

695. 表达 /biǎo dá/ - to express

696. 算 /suàn/ - to calculate

697. 浪费 /làng fèi/ - to waste

698. 保护 /bǎo hù/ - to protect; to defend; protection

699. 代表 /dài biǎo/ - to represent; representative

700. 安排 /ān pái/ - to arrange

701. 反映 /fǎn yìng/ - to reflect; reflex

他们的行动清楚地反映了他们的思想。- Their actions clearly reflect their thoughts.

法律应该是人民意志的反映。- The law should represent the will of the people.

702. 讨论 /tǎo lùn/ - to discuss

703. 改变 /gǎi biàn/ - to change; to alter

704. 超过 /chāo guò/ - to surpass; to exceed

705. 放弃 /fàng qì/ - to give up

706. 调查 /diào chá/ - to investigate; investigation

707. 照 /zhào/ - to shine; to look in the mirror; to take (photo); as (requested, etc.)

他用手电筒往地窖各处照了照。- He shone the flashlight around the cellar.

我照了照镜子,看见自己满脸是汗。- I looked in the mirror and saw that my face was covered in sweat.

能不能帮我照张像? - Could you please take a photo for me?

照我说的做。- Do as I say.

708. 联系 /lián xì/ - to link; to contact; contact; connection

709. 停 /tíng/ - to stop; to halt; to park (a car)

710. 停止 /tíng zhǐ/ - to stop

711. 缺少 /quē shǎo/ - to lack; to be short of
712. 通知 /tōng zhī/ - to notify; to inform; notice; notification
713. 翻译 /fān yì/ - to translate; translator; translation
714. 组织 /zǔ zhī/ - to organize; organization
715. 发展 /fā zhǎn/ - to develop; development
716. 阅读 /yuè dú/ - to read; reading
717. 鼓励 /gǔ lì/ - to encourage
718. 预习 /yù xí/ - to prepare a lesson
719. 访问 /fǎng wèn/ - to visit; to interview; visit
720. 信任 /xìn rèn/ - to trust; to believe in
721. 坚持 /jiān chí/ - to insist on; to persist; persistence
722. 受到 /shòu dào/ - to suffer
723. 重视 /zhòng shì/ - to attach importance to something; to value
724. 复印 /fù yìn/ - to photocopy
725. 打印 /dǎ yìn/ - to print
726. 打扰 /dǎ rǎo/ - to disturb; to bother; to interrupt; to trouble
727. 打招呼 /dǎ zhāo hu/ - to greet someone
728. 扩大 /kuò dà/ - to expand; expansion
729. 整理 /zhěng lǐ/ - to collate (data; files); to tidy up; to sort out
730. 组成 /zǔ chéng/ - to consist of
731. 参观 /cān guān/ - to look around
732. 集合 /jí hé/ - to gather
733. 总结 /zǒng jié/ - to sum up; to conclude; summary
734. 节约 /jiē yuē/ - to economize; to conserve (resources)
735. 放松 /fàng sōng/ - to relax
736. 限制 /xiàn zhì/ - to restrict; to restrain; restriction
737. 请假 /qǐng jià/ - to ask for time off
738. 放暑假 /fàng shǔ jià/ - to take a summer vacation
739. 负责 /fù zé/ - to be responsible for; to take responsibility for
740. 证明 /zhèng míng/ - to prove; to testify; proof

741. 广播/guǎng bō/ - to broadcast; broadcast

742. 保证/bǎo zhèng/ - to guarantee; to ensure; guarantee

743. 代替/dài tì/ - to replace

744. 毕业/bì yè/ - to graduate; graduation

745. 请客/qǐng kè/ - treat

今天我请客。- I'm treating (you) today. (It's on me today.)

746. 申请/shēn qǐng/ - to apply; application

747. 出发/chū fā/ - to set off; to start out

748. 污染/wū rǎn/ - pollution; to contaminate

749. 出差/chū chāi/ - to go on a business trip

750. 报名/bào míng/ - to sign up

751. 约会/yuē huì/ - appointment; date

752. 邀请/yāo qǐng/ - to invite; invitation

753. 理发/lǐ fā/ - to get a haircut

754. 估计/gū jì/ - to estimate

755. 解释/jiě shì/ - to explain; explanation

756. 说明/shuō míng/ - to explain; to illustrate; instruction

757. 理解/lǐ jiě/ - to comprehend; to understand; comprehension; understanding

758. 聊天/liáo tiān/ - to chat

759. 竞争/jìng zhēng/ - to compete; competition

760. 打折/dǎ zhé/ - to give a discount

761. 打扮/dǎ bàn/ - to dress up; manner of dressing

762. 招聘/zhāo pìn/ - to invite applications for a job; recruitment

763. 出生/chū shēng/ - to be born

764. 制造/zhì zào/ - to manufacture

765. 包括/bāo kuò/ - to include

766. 符合/fú hé/ - in accordance with; to agree with; to correspond with; to conform to

767. 行/xíng/ - to do; to perform; all right; OK; acceptable

这个方案简单易行。- This plan is simple and easy to perform.

行，就这么定了。- OK, it's settled.

她教英语行吗？- Is she competent at teaching English?

/háng/ - line; row

请站成一行。- Please stand in one row.

我对此不打在行。- That's not much in my line.

768. 例如/lì rú/ - such as; for example; for instance; e.g.

769. 受不了/shòu bu liǎo/ - can't stand; unbearable

770. 做生意/zuò shēng yì/ - to do business

771. 弹钢琴/tán gāng qín/ - to play the piano

772. 开玩笑/kāi wán xiào/ - to joke

773. 醒/xǐng/ - to wake up; to awaken; to be awake

774. 响/xiǎng/ - to make a sound; to sound; loud

775. 积累/jī lèi/ - to accumulate; accumulation

776. 禁止/jìn zhǐ/ - to prohibit; to forbid; to ban

777. 推迟/tuī chí/ - to postpone; to put off

778. 干杯/gān bēi/ - Cheers! (proposing a toast); Bottoms up!

779. 祝贺/zhù hè/ - to congratulate; congratulations

780. 回忆/huí yì/ - to recall; recollection

781. 免费/miǎn fèi/ - free (of charge)

782. 谈/tán/ - to talk

783. 提醒/tí xǐng/ - to remind

784. 来不及/lái bù jí/ - there's not enough time (to do something); it's too late (to do something)

785. 来得及/lái de jí/ - there's still time; able to do something in time

786. 误会/wù huì/ - to misunderstand; misunderstanding

787. 同情/tóng qíng/ - to show sympathy for; to sympathize; compassion

788. 不得不/bù dé bù/ - have to

我不得不走了。- I have to go.

789. 加班/jiā bān/ - to work overtime

790. 帮忙/bāng máng/ - to help; to do a favor

791. 乘坐/chéng zuò/ - to ride (in a vehicle, train, plane, ship, etc.)

792. 购物/gòu wù/ - to go shopping

793. 起飞/qǐ fēi/ - to take off

794. 收/shōu/ - to receive; to collect

795. 减肥/jiǎn féi/ - to lose weight

796. 交/jiāo/ - to hand over; to make (friends); to pay (money)

797. 允许/yǔn xǔ/ - to permit; to allow; permission

798. 判断/pàn duàn/ - to judge; judgment

799. 排列/pái liè/ - to line; to rank; permutation

800. 爱/ài/ - to love; love

801. 喜欢/xǐ huān/ - to like

802. 想/xiǎng/ - to think; to wish; to want; to miss

我想我得走了。- I think I need to go.

我想有个假期。- I want to go on holiday.

他想去博物馆。- He wants to go to the museum.

她想家了。- She misses her home. (She is homesick.)

803. 认识/rèn shi/ - to know; to realize; to understand.

我认识这个地方。- I know this place.

他已经认识到自己的过错了。- He has realized the mistakes he made.

请谈谈你对这件事的认识。- Please talk about your understanding of this matter.

804. 觉得/jué de/ - to think; to feel

805. 知道/zhī dào/ - to know; to be aware of

806. 希望/xī wàng/ - to wish; to hope; hope

我希望我能做那件事。- I wish I could do that.

我希望你会成为我们的靠山。- I hope that you will become our patron.

有生命就有希望。- Where there is life, there is hope.

807. 祝/zhù/ - to wish; to hope

祝你成功！- (I) wish you success!

祝你健康！- (I) hope you are well!

808. 关心/guān xīn/ - to care; to be concerned

809. 担心/dān xīn/ - to worry; to be worried

810. 烦恼/fán nǎo/ - to worry; trouble

不要为小事烦恼。- Don't worry over trifles.

有什么事情让你烦恼吗？- Is anything troubling you?

咱们忘掉那些烦恼吧。- Let's forget about those troubles.

811. 放心/fàng xīn/ - to be at ease; to set one's mind at rest

812. 小心/xiǎo xīn/ - to be careful; to watch out

813. 害怕/hài pà/ - to be afraid; to be scared

814. 相信/xiàng xìn/ - to believe

815. 记得/jì dé/ - to remember

816. 努力/nǔ lì/ - to try hard; to make great effort

817. 使/shǐ/ - to use; to make

我能使一下你的笔吗？- May I use your pen for a while?

什么使你这么想呢？- What makes you think so?

818. 讨厌/tǎo yàn/ - to dislike; to hate; annoying

819. 后悔/hòu huǐ/ - to regret

820. 失望/shī wàng/ - to despair; disappointed

821. 羡慕/xiàn mù/ - to admire; to envy

822. 怀疑/huái yí/ - to suspect; to doubt; suspicion

823. 感谢/gǎn xiè/ - (to express) thanks; gratitude

非常感谢你能加入。- Thank you for joining us.

824. 原谅/yuán liàng/ - to forgive; to excuse; to pardon; forgiveness

825. 支持/zhī chí/ - to support; to stand by; support

826. 尊重/zūn zhòng/ - to honor; to respect; respect

827. 反对/fǎn duì/ - to fight against; to oppose; opposition

828. 考虑/kǎo lǜ/ - to think over; consideration

Auxiliary verbs occur before a verb and express the meanings of possibility, ability, permission, obligation, and prohibition.

829. 会/huì/ - can; to be able to; will; to meet; meeting; a moment

我会说中文。- I can speak Chinese.

我会骑马。- I'm able to ride a horse.

他会来吗？- Will he come?

830. 她要到公园会男朋友。- She's going to the party to meet her boyfriend.

今下午有个会要开。- I have a meeting to attend in the afternoon.

我一会就来。- I'll come in a moment.

831. 能/néng/ - can; to be able to; to be capable of

我能自己去。- I can go by myself.

你明天能来吗？- Are you able to come tomorrow?

我自己能行。- I'm capable of doing it alone.

832. 可以/kě yǐ/ - can; may

我们可以帮助你。- We can help you.

我可以抽烟吗？- May I smoke a cigarette here?

833. 要/yào/ - need; be going to; to want; to take

你要好好学习。- You need to study hard.

天要下雨。- It's going to rain.

我要回家。- I want to go home.

我要了。- I'll take it.

834. 可能/kě néng/ - might; maybe; possible; possibly; possibility

我以为你可能已经邀请他过来了。- I thought you might have invited him over.

我可能错了。- Maybe I was wrong.
有可能。- It's possible.
我不可能放弃工作。- I couldn't possibly give up work.
我的确想过有失败的可能。- The possibility of failure did cross my mind.

835. 应该/yīng gāi/ - should; ought to

836. 愿意/yuàn yì/ - will; to be willing to
你愿意和我换一下座位吗？- Will you change seats with me?
他很愿意找我的要价付钱。- He's quite willing to pay the price I ask.

837. 敢/gǎn/ - to dare
他们怎么敢做出这样的事？- How dare they do such a thing?

Chapter 3. Pronouns and Adjectives

Chinese pronouns are not distinguished in terms of grammatical roles. The same pronouns are used for subject, object, possession, etc. Some pronouns have singular and plural forms. The suffix -们/men/ is added to the singular form to turn it into the plural form. In addition, gender is not reflected in the spoken language. The written language has distinctions for second- and third-person pronouns, though only the third-person gender distinction is commonly used.

838. 我/wǒ/ – I; me

839. 你/nǐ/ – you (singular; informal)

840. 您/nín/ – you (singular; formal)

841. 他/tā/ – he; him; (used for either sex when the sex is unknown or unimportant)

842. 她/tā/ – she; her

843. 它/tā/ – it

844. 我们/wǒ men/ – we; us

845. 咱们/zán men/ – we; us (colloquial)

846. 这(这儿)/zhè (zhèr)/ – this; those; here

847. 那(那儿)/nà (nàer)/ – that; those; there

848. 哪(哪儿)/nǎ (nǎer)/ - where; which

849. 谁/shuí/ - who; whom

850. 什么/shén me/ - what

851. 多少/duō shǎo/ - how much; how many
桌子上有多少个苹果？- How many apples are on the table?
你还有多少钱？- How much money do you have?

852. 几/jǐ/ - how much; how many; several; a few
我几天前来的。- I came here several days ago.
我就呆几天。- I just stay for a few days.

853. 怎么/zěn me/ - how

854. 怎么样/zěn me yàng/ - how about; what about

855. 大家/dà jiā/ - everyone

856. 为什么/wèi shén me/ - why

857. 自己/zì jǐ/ - self; own

858. 别人/bié rén/ - other people

859. 其他/qí tā/ - other; else

860. 一切/yí qiè/ - everything; all

861. 任何/rèn hé/ - whatever; whichever; whatsoever

862. 每/měi/ - every; each

863. 各/gè/ - each; every

Adjectives describe the shape or property of a person or thing or the state of a movement or action. In Chinese, the form of an adjective remains unchanged in all circumstances.

864. 好/hǎo/ - good; well; fine; very; easy to
我很好。- I'm fine.
我好高兴。- I'm very happy.
她是一个好相处的人。- She's easy to get along with.

865. 大/dà/ - big; huge; large; old
我喜欢住大房子。- I like to live in a big house.
她比我大两岁。- She is two years older than me.

866. 小/xiǎo/ - small; tiny; young

这双鞋子太小了。- This pair of shoes is too small.

我比她小三岁。- I'm three years younger than her.

867. 多/duō/ - a lot of; more; many; much

我的积蓄不多了。- I don't have many savings.

他的收入比我多。- He earns more than me.

868. 少/shǎo/ - few; little

869. 冷/lěng/ - cold

870. 热/rè/ - hot (of weather); to heat

今天真热。- What a hot day today.

请帮我把鸡汤热一下。- Please heat up the chicken soup for me.

871. 高兴/gāo xìng/ - happy; glad; willing (to do something)

872. 漂亮/piào liàng/ - beautiful; pretty

873. 高/gāo/ - high; tall; Gao (surname)

874. 红/hóng/ - red

875. 白/bái/ - white; Bai (surname)

876. 黑/hēi/ - black; dark

877. 忙/máng/ - busy

878. 快/kuài/ - fast; quick; sharp (of knives or wits)

879. 慢/màn/ - slow

880. 远/yuǎn/ - far

881. 近/jìn/ - near; close to

882. 好吃/hǎo chī/ - tasty; delicious

883. 累/lèi/ - tired

884. 长/cháng/ - long; length

它脖子很长。- Its neck is long.

它长约一米。- It's about a meter in length.

/zhǎng/ - to grow

这孩子一年不见，长这么高了。- It's only a year since I saw the child last time and he's grown so tall.

885. 新/xīn/ - new

886. 贵/guì/ - expensive

887. 便宜/pián yi/ - cheap; inexpensive

888. 晴/qíng/ - fine (weather); sunny

889. 阴/yīn/ - cloudy; Yin (of Yin and Yang); negative (electric)

890. 错/cuò/ - wrong; fault

我错了。- I was wrong.

这是我的错。- It's my fault.

891. 快乐/kuài lè/ - happy

892. 蓝/lán/ - blue

893. 绿/lǜ/ - green

894. 黄/huáng/ - yellow; Huang (surname)

895. 低/dī/ - low; beneath; too low

896. 矮/ǎi/ - low; short (in height)

897. 短/duǎn/ - short (in length)

898. 久/jiǔ/ - (long) time; (long) duration of time

899. 旧/jiù/ - old (of things); worn (with age)

900. 老/lǎo/ - old (of people); tough (of meat, etc.)

901. 容易/róng yì/ - easy

902. 难/nán/ - difficult

/nàn/ - disaster

903. 坏/huài/ - bad; broken; to break down

904. 甜/tián/ - sweet

905. 饱/bǎo/ - to be full

906. 空/kōng/ - empty; vacant

/kòng/ - space; to be free

你有空吗？- Are you free?

仓库里还有空吗？- Is there any space in the warehouse?

907. 相同/xiàng tóng/ - same; identical

908. 简单/jiǎn dān/ - simple; easy

909. 一样/yí yàng/ - the same as; same; just like; equal to

910. 有名/yǒu míng/ - famous; well known

911. 重要/zhòng yào/ - important; significant

912. 全部/quán bù/ - whole; entire

913. 一般/yì bān/ - ordinary; common; generally; in general

914. 清楚/qīng chǔ/ - clear; distinct; clearly; to be clear about

915. 安静/ān jìng/ - quiet

916. 方便/fāng biàn/ - convenient; to help out (to make things easy for people); (euphemism) to go to the toilet

在你方便的时候请联系我。- Please contact me when it is convenient for you.

能不能行个方便？- Could you please help me out?

我需要去方便一下。- I need to go to the toilet.

917. 干净/gàn jìng/ - clean

918. 新鲜/xīn xiān/ - fresh (air, fruit, etc.)

919. 奇怪/qí guài/ - strange; odd

920. 胖/pàng/ - fat

921. 瘦/shòu/ - tight; thin

这件裤子太瘦了。- The pants are tight.

她很瘦。- She's thin.

922. 舒服/shū fu/ - comfortable

923. 健康/jiàn kāng/ - healthy; health

924. 饿/è/ - hungry

925. 渴/kě/ - thirsty

926. 年轻/nián qīng/ - young

927. 聪明/cōng míng/ - intelligent; smart

928. 可爱/kě ài/ - cute; lovely

929. 认真/rèn zhēn/ - conscientious; earnest; to take seriously

930. 热情/rè qíng/ - enthusiastic; passionate; passion; passionately

931. 难过/nán guò/ - sad; upset

932. 着急/zhe jí/ - anxious; to worry

933. 紧张/jǐn zhāng/ - nervous

934. 突然/tū rán/ - sudden; suddenly

935. 主要/zhǔ yào/ - main; major

936. 合适/hé shì/ - suitable; to fit

937. 假/jiǎ/ - fake

938. 富/fù/ - rich

939. 穷/qióng/ - poor

940. 轻/qīng/ - light (of weight); gentle; soft

941. 重/zhòng/ - heavy

942. 宽/kuān/ - wide; broad

943. 窄/zhǎi/ - narrow

944. 粗心/cū xīn/ - careless; thoughtless

945. 干燥/gàn zào/ - dry

946. 湿润/shī rùn/ - moist

947. 深/shēn/ - deep; dark (of color, water, etc.); late (of night)

948. 硬/yìng/ - tough; hard

他的心肠一定很硬。- His heart must be very hard.

那牛排硬得他没法吃。- The steak was so tough that he couldn't eat it.

949. 软/ruǎn/ - soft

950. 苦/kǔ/ - bitter

951. 咸/xián/ - salty

952. 酸/suān/ - sour

953. 辣/là/ - spicy

954. 暗/àn/ - dark; dim

955. 亮/liàng/ - bright

956. 安全/ān quán/ - safe; secure

957. 危险/wēi xiǎn/ - dangerous; danger

958. 暖和/nuǎn huo/ - warm

959. 凉快/liáng kuài/ - cool

960. 美丽/měi lì/ - beautiful

961. 整齐/zhěng qí/ - neat; in good order

962. 乱/luàn/ - disordered; in a mess

963. 脏/zāng/ - dirty

964. 帅/shuài/ - handsome

965. 圆/yuán/ - round; circular; circle

966. 棒/bàng/ - smart; amazing; strong (of body); rod

你真棒！- You're smart.

太棒了！- That's wonderful!

他的身体很棒。- His body is strong.

967. 紧张/jǐn zhāng/ - nervous

968. 轻松/qīng sōng/ - relaxed; relaxing

969. 冷静/lěng jìng/ - calm

970. 幸福/xìng fú/ - happiness; wellbeing

971. 愉快/yú kuài/ - delighted; pleasing; delightful

972. 感兴趣/gǎn xìng qù/ - to be interested

973. 兴奋/xīng fèn/ - exciting; excited

974. 吃惊/chī jīng/ - to be shocked

975. 可惜/kě xī/ - it is a pity; what a pity

976. 困/kùn/ - to be trapped; to be sleepy

977. 笨/bèn/ - stupid; foolish; silly

978. 诚实/chéng shí/ - honest; honesty

979. 勇敢/yǒng gǎn/ - brave

980. 优秀/yōu xiù/ - outstanding; excellent

981. 骄傲/jiāo ào/ - proud

982. 害羞/hài xiū/ - shy

983. 激动/jī dòng/ - exciting; excited

984. 感动/gǎn dòng/ - moving; to move (someone); to touch (someone emotionally)

这是一个感人的故事。- This is a moving story.

她被他的真心感动了。- She was moved by his sincerity.

985. 活泼/huó pō/ - active; lively

986. 懒/lǎn/ - lazy

987. 辛苦/xīn kǔ/ - exhausting; exhausted

988. 成熟/chéng shú/ - mature

989. 热闹/rè nao/ - bustling (with noise and excitement)

990. 孤单/gū dān/ - alone; lonely

991. 吵/chǎo/ - noisy; to argue; to disturb by making noise

你好吵！- You are so noisy!

别吵了！- Stop arguing!

别吵我！- Don't disturb me!

992. 耐心/nài xīn/ - to be patient; patience

993. 仔细/zǐ xì/ - careful; cautious

994. 友好/yǒu hǎo/ - friendly

995. 可怜/kě lián/ - pathetic; to pity

不要可怜死者。可怜活人，尤其是那些生活中没有爱的人。- Do not pity the dead. Pity the living, and above all, those who live without love.

996. 严重/yán zhòng/ - serious; severe

997. 无聊/wú liáo/ - bored; boring

998. 香/xiāng/ - fragrant; aromatic

999. 严格/yán gé/ - strict

1000. 故意/gù yì/ - to be on purpose; deliberately

1001. 随便/suí biàn/ - casual; as one wishes

1002. 精彩/jīng cǎi/ - splendid

1003. 复杂/fù zá/ - complex; complicated

1004. 详细/xiáng xì/ - detailed; in detail

1005. 丰富/fēng fù/ - abundant

1006. 流利/liú lì/ - fluent

1007. 有趣/yǒu qù/ - interesting; interested

1008. 麻烦/má fan/ - inconvenient; trouble; to trouble or bother someone

这是一件麻烦事。- This is an inconvenient thing.

你给我们造成了很多麻烦。- You've caused us a lot of trouble.

不好意思麻烦你。- Sorry to bother you.

1009. 肯定/kěn dìng/ - to confirm; to be sure; to be certain; sure; certain; affirmative

1010. 流行/liú xíng/ - popular; to rage (of contagious disease)

1011. 直接/zhí jiē/ - direct; directly

1012. 许多/xǔ duō/ - a great deal of; many; much; a lot of

1013. 满/mǎn/ - full; fill; to reach the limit; to fill; surname

他满脑子荒唐想法。- His head is full of nonsense.

再给你满上一杯。- Let me fill your glass once more.

缸里盛满了酒。- The crock is filled with wine.

1014. 完全/wán quán/ - whole; complete; totally; entirely

1015. 所有/suǒ yǒu/ - all; to possess; to own

1016. 普遍/pǔ biàn/ - widespread

1017. 厉害/lì hài/ - awesome; terrible; ferocious

1018. 准确/zhǔn què/ - accurate; exact; precise

1019. 著名/zhù míng/ - famous; well known

1020. 正好/zhèng hǎo/ - just (in time); just right; just enough

1021. 够/gòu/ - to be enough

1022. 差不多/chà bu duō/ - almost; nearly; more or less

1023. 及时/jí shí/ - in time; promptly; timely

1024. 准时/zhǔn shí/ - on time

1025. 专门/zhuān mén/ - specialized

1026. 正式/zhèng shì/ - formal; official

1027. 合格 /hé gé/ - qualified

1028. 正确 /zhèng què/ - correct

1029. 对 /duì/ - right; correct; towards

你是对的。- You are right.

她热情地对我们伸出双手。- She warmly extended her hands towards us.

1030. 真正 /zhēn zhèng/ - real; genuine; genuinely

1031. 高级 /gāo jí/ - fancy

1032. 正常 /zhèng cháng/ - normal

1033. 原来 /yuán lái/ - original; originally; to turn out

原来是你！- It was you!

1034. 永远 /yǒng yuǎn/ - forever; eternal; eternity

1035. 暂时 /zàn shí/ - temporary; temporarily

1036. 相反 /xiàng fǎn/ - opposite; contrary

1037. 熟悉 /shú xī/ - to be familiar with; to know well

1038. 破 /pò/ - worn out; to be broken; to be damaged

1039. 马虎 /mǎ hu/ - careless

1040. 另外 /lìng wài/ - additional; in addition; furthermore

1041. 难受 /nán shòu/ - to feel unwell; to feel ill

1042. 伤心 /shāng xīn/ - sad; to feel deeply hurt

1043. 积极 /jī jí/ - proactive; positive; vigorous

1044. 共同 /gòng tóng/ - common; together; jointly

1045. 浪漫 /làng màn/ - romantic

1046. 得意 /dé yì/ - to be proud or pleased of oneself

1047. 现代 /xiàn dài/ - modern

1048. 幽默 /yōu mò/ - humorous; humor

1049. 本来 /běn lái/ - original; originally

Chapter 4. Numerals and Measure Words

1050. 零/líng/ - zero
1051. 一/yī/ - one
1052. 二/èr/ - two
1053. 三/sān/ - three
1054. 四/sì/ - four
1055. 五/wǔ/ - five
1056. 六/liù/ - six
1057. 七/qī/ - seven
1058. 八/bā/ - eight
1059. 九/jiǔ/ - nine
1060. 十/shí/ - ten
1061. 百/bǎi/ - hundred; Bai (surname)
1062. 千/qiān/ - thousand
1063. 万/wàn/ - ten thousand;
1064. 亿/yì/ - hundred million
1065. 两/liǎng/ - two (quantities); both; weight equal to 50 grams
1066. 俩/liǎ/ - two (quantities, colloquial); both (colloquial)

1067. 半/bàn/ - half

In English, mass nouns such as "coffee", "rice", and "sand" occur with measure words. In Chinese, all nouns occur with measure words when they are preceded by a specifier and/or number. Therefore, it is imperative when learning Chinese to learn every noun with its matching measure word.

1068. 个/gè/ - measure word for people or objects in general

1069. 岁/suì/ - measure word for years of age

1070. 本/běn/ - measure word for books, periodicals, files, etc.

1071. 些/xiē/ - measure word for people or objects in general; some; few; several

1072. 块/kuài/ - measure word for pieces of cloth, cake, etc.; *yuan* (colloquial)

1073. 次/cì/ - measure word for enumerated events; time; (inferior quality)

下次见！- See you next time!

这件衬衫很次。- The quality of this shirt is poor.

1074. 公斤/gōng jīn/ - kilogram (measure unit)

1075. 元/yuán/ - *yuan* (monetary unit); Yuan (surname)

1076. 件/jiàn/ - measure word for events, things, clothes, etc.

1077. 张/zhāng/ - measure word for flat objects, sheet, votes, etc.; Zhang (surname)

1078. 角/jiǎo/ - 10 cents (monetary unit); horn; angle; corner

1079. 分/fēn/ - cent (monetary unit); minute (time unit); score (in sports or games)

1080. 条/tiáo/ - measure word for long, thin things (ribbon, river, road, pants, etc.); clause (of law or treaty); strip

1081. 位/wèi/ - measure word for binary bits, customers, members, etc.

1082. 双/shuāng/ - measure word for socks, shoes, chopsticks, etc.; pair; double; two

1083. 辆/liàng/ - measure word for vehicles

1084. 层/céng/ - layer; floor (of a building); measure word for layers

1085. 座/zuò/ - measure word for buildings, mountains, etc.; seat

1086. 台/tái/ - measure word for vehicles, machines, etc.; broadcasting station

1087. 份/fèn/ - measure word for gifts, newspapers, magazines, papers, reports, contracts, etc.; share; copy;

1089. 篇/piān/ - measure word for written items

1090. 朵/duǒ/ - measure word for flowers

1091. 棵/kē/ - measure word for trees, cabbages, plants, etc.

1092. 公里/gōng lǐ/ - kilometer (measure unit)

1093. 场/chǎng/ - measure word for races, matches, activities, exams, etc.; a ground where ball games are played

1094. 群/qún/ - a group of

1095. 趟/tàng/ - measure word for trips, runs made, etc.

Chapter 5. Adverbs, Prepositions, and Conjunctions

Adverbs are generally used in front of a verb or an adjective to express time, degree, scope, repetition, negation, possibility or tone of speech, etc. Adverbs add many different kinds of meaning to a sentence.

1096. 不/bù/ - not (negative prefix); no

中文语法并不难。- Chinese grammar isn't hard.

你喜欢这个吗？不。- Do you like this? No.

1097. 很/hěn/ - very; quite

1098. 太/tài/ - too (much, many); very; extremely

1099. 都/dōu/ - all; both; already; even

所有人都过来。- All of you, come here.

我们两个都去过北京。- Both of us have been to Beijing.

我都走了！- I have already gone!

你都没去！- You didn't even go there!

1100. 别/bié/ - do not; must not; to pin

别动！- Don't move.

她在头发上别了一支鲜花。- She pinned a flower to her hair.

1101. 非常/fēi cháng/ - very; extreme

1102. 也/yě/ - also; too

1103. 最/zuì/ - most; the most

1104. 左右/zuǒ yòu/ - approximately; about; left and right; to be controlled

1105. 正在/zhèng zài/ - in the process of (doing something or happening)

他正在睡觉。- He is sleeping.

1106. 已经/yǐ jīng/ - already

1107. 一起/yī qǐ/ - together; in the same place; with; altogether

1108. 再/zài/ - once more; again

欢迎下次再来。- You're welcome back again.

1109. 又/yòu/ - again

1110. 只有/zhǐ yǒu/...才/cái/... - only if... then...

1111. 更/gèng/ - more; even more

1112. 越/yuè/ - the more...

1113. 特别/tè bié/ - especially; special; particular

1114. 比较/bǐ jiào/ - rather; comparatively; to compare

1115. 比如/bǐ rú/ - such as; for example; for instance; e.g.

1116. 一直/yì zhí/ - straight; continuously; always

1117. 总是/zǒng shì/ - always

1118. 经常/jīng cháng/ - often; regularly

1119. 终于/zhōng yú/ - at last; in the end; finally; eventually

1120. 当然/dāng rán/ - of course; certainly; absolutely

1121. 其实/qí shí/ - actually; in fact

1122. 几乎/jǐ hū/ - almost; nearly

1123. 一定/yí dìng/ - surely; certainly; must

1124. 多么/duō me/ - how (wonderful, etc.); what (a great idea, etc.); however (difficult it is, etc.)

天空是多么晴朗！- How clear the sky is!

多么奇妙的点子！- What an amazing thought!

无论多么困难，我都要坚持下去。- No matter how difficult it is, I will stick with it to the end.

1125. 马上/mǎ shàng/ - immediately; right away; at once

1126. 必须/bì xū/ - must; have to; compulsory

1127. 十分/shí fèn/ - very; extremely; ten points

1128. 尤其/yóu qí/ - especially; particularly

1129. 挺/tǐng/ - quite; to straighten up; very; to stand up for; measure word for machine guns

我今天过得挺开行。- I'm quite happy today.

我叫他们挺起身子来。- I told them to straighten up.

我挺你！- I stand up for you!

1130. 大概/dà gài/ -- roughly; probably; rough; approximate; about

1131. 大约/dà yuē/ - approximately; about

1132. 也许/yě xǔ/ - perhaps; maybe; probably

1133. 恐怕/kǒng pà/ - perhaps; maybe; to be afraid that

1134. 难道/nán dào/ - could it be said that

1135. 只好/zhī hǎo/ - without any better option; to have to; to be forced to

1136. 最好/zuì hǎo/ - best; had better

1137. 仍然/réng rán/ - still; yet

1138. 竟然/jìng rán/ - unexpectedly

1139. 到底/dào dǐ/ - finally; in the end; when all is said and done; after all; to the last

1140. 却/què/ - but; however; yet

1141. 首先/shǒu xiān/ - first of all; in the first place

1142. 其次/qí cì/ - next; secondly

1143. 最后/zuì hòu/ - finally; last; final

1144. 刚/gāng/ - just; barely

1145. 忽然/hū rán/ - suddenly

1146. 连/lián/ - to link; to connect; even; company (military)

1147. 从来/cóng lái/ – always; at all time; never (if used in a negative sentence)

他从来都是一个人吃午饭。– He always ate lunch alone.

我从来不去公厕。– I never go to the public toilet.

1148. 按时/àn shí/ – on time; on schedule

1149. 重新/chóng xīn/ – again; once more

你需要重新开始。– You need to start again.

他重新讲了一遍。– He explained it once more.

1150. 至少/zhì shǎo/ – at least

1151. 到处/dào chù/ – in all places; everywhere

1152. 互相/hù xiàng/ – each other

1153. 顺便/shùn biàn/ – without extra effort

1154. 确实/què shí/ – indeed; really

1155. 偶尔/ǒu ěr/ – occasionally; once in a while

1156. 究竟/jiū jìng/ – after all (when all is said and done)

1157. 稍微/shāo wēi/ – a little bit

1158. 甚至/shèn zhì/ – so much so that; even

1159. 往往/wǎng wǎng/ – often; frequently

Conjunctions are words that join phrases belonging to the same grammatical category and indicate a relationship like coordination, causality, condition, supposition, etc.

1160. 和/hé/ – and; with

1161. 因为/yīn wéi/ – because

1162. 所以/suǒ yǐ/ – so; therefore

1163. 但是/dàn shì/ – but; however

1164. 虽然/suī rán/ – although, though

1165. 然后/rán hòu/ – then; after that

1166. 如果/rú guǒ/ – if; in case; in the event that

1167. 一边/yì biān/ – on the one hand; one side

1168. 或者/huò zhě/ – or; maybe; perhaps

1169. 还是 /hái shì/ – or; nevertheless
1170. 不仅 /bù jǐn/ – not only
1171. 不但 /bú dàn/ – not only
1172. 而且 /ér qiě/ – but also
1173. 然而 /rán ér/ – however; but; yet
1174. 可是 /kě shì/ – but; however
1175. 不过 /bú guò/ – but; however; only; no more than

我可以去，不过你得跟我一起。– I'll go, but you have to go with me.

他不过是一个部门经理。– He's only a department manager.

这座城市不过三十万人。– There are no more than 300,000 people in this city.

1176. 只要 /zhǐ yào/ – if only; as long as
1177. 不管 /bù guǎn/ – regardless of; no matter (what, when, how, which)
1178. 无论 /wú lùn/ – no matter what; no matter how; regardless of
1179. 并且 /bìng qiě/ – moreover; furthermore
1180. 因此 /yīn cǐ/ – as a result; consequently
1181. 于是 /yú shì/ – hence; as a result; consequently
1182. 否则 /fǒu zé/ – if not; otherwise
1183. 即使 /jí shǐ/ – even if; even though
1184. 尽管 /jìn guǎn/ – despite; although; even though; do not hesitate (to ask, complain, etc.); (go ahead and do something) without hesitating
1185. 而 /ér/ – but; and; (indicates changes of state, contrast, causal relation, etc.)

Prepositions can be put before a noun or pronoun to form a prepositional phrase indicating time, place, direction, object, reason, manner, the passive, companion, exclusion, etc.

1186. 在 /zài/ – (located) at; (to be) in; (indicating an action in progress)

1187. 从/cóng/ - from; via

1188. 比/bǐ/ - used for comparison; to gesture (with hands); ratio
我比他高。- I'm taller than him.
她朝服务员比了一个手势。- She gestured to the waiter.
下面的图表显示了个人负债与收入之比。- The bottom chart shows the ratio of personal debt to personal income.

1189. 离/lí/ - (in giving distances) from
这里离火车站多远？- How far from here to the train station?

1190. 为了/wèi le/ - in order to; so as to

1191. 除了/chú le/ - except; in addition to; apart from

1192. 被/bèi/ - by (indicates passive-voice sentences or clauses)

1193. 关于/guān yú/ - with regards to; about; concerning

1194. 经过/jīng guò/ - after; to go through; to pass

1195. 往/wǎng/ - to or towards (a direction or a place)

1196. 由于/yóu yú/ - as a result of; owing to; due to; because

1197. 对于/duì yú/ - with regards to; regarding

1198. 按照/àn zhào/ - according to; in accordance with

1199. 随着/suí zhe/ - along with

1200. 跟/gēn/ - with; to

PART II
LEARN 1,300 OTHER WORDS

This part will require you to have mastered a large number of words and sentence patterns. Some are more often used in oral language, and some in written forms. This part also has higher requirements in speaking, reading, listening, and writing.

Be patient and look for shortcuts by grasping the key points. Though the content in this part may be overwhelming, some words are basic and commonly used. As they are fundamentals, they will require your careful attention.

Chapter 6. Nouns (A ~ Q)

1201. 报社/bào shè/ - newspaper office
1202. 岸/àn/ - shore
1203. 爱心/ài xīn/ - compassion
1204. 傍晚/bàng wǎn/ - at dusk; nightfall
1205. 包裹/bāo guǒ/ - package; parcel; to wrap up
1206. 宝贝/bǎo bèi/ - baby; treasure
1207. 保险/bǎo xiǎn/ - insurance; to insure
1208. 报告/bào gào/ - report; to report
1209. 背景/bèi jǐng/ - background
1210. 被子/bèi zi/ - quilt
1211. 本科/běn kē/ - undergraduate course; undergraduate
1212. 本领/běn lǐng/ - skill; ability; capability
他的本领就是这么得来的。- This is how he acquired his skill.
1213. 本质/běn zhì/ - nature; essence
有人可能认为抽烟从本质上说就具有成瘾性。- One could argue that smoking, by its very nature, is addictive.
1214. 比例/bǐ lì/ - proportion
1215. 鞭炮/biān pào/ - firecracker
1216. 标点/biāo diǎn/ - punctuation

1217. 标志/biāo zhì/ - sign; mark; symbol; to indicate; to mark
这标志着人类历史新纪元的开始。- It marks the beginning of a new era in human history.

1218. 表面/biǎo miàn/ - surface

1219. 表情/biǎo qíng/ - expression

1220. 冰激凌/bīng jī líng/ - ice cream

1221. 病毒/bìng dú/ - virus

1222. 玻璃/bō li/ - glass

1223. 博物馆/bó wù guǎn/ - museum

1224. 脖子/bó zi/ - neck

1225. 布/bù/ - cloth

1226. 部门/bù mén/ - department

1227. 步骤/bù zhòu/ - step

1228. 财产/cái chǎn/ - property; assets

1229. 彩虹/cǎi hóng/ - rainbow

1230. 参考/cān kǎo/ - reference; to refer

1231. 操场/cāo chǎng/ - playground

1232. 叉子/chā zi/ - folk

1233. 差距/chā jù/ - disparity

1234. 产品/chǎnpǐn/ - product; merchandise

1235. 长途/chángtú/ - long distance

1236. 常识/chángshí/ - common sense

1237. 车库/chē kù/ - garage

1238. 车厢/chē xiāng/ - carriage

1239. 程度/chéng dù/ - degree; extent

1240. 程序/chéng xù/ - procedure; computer program

1241. 成分/chéng fèn/ - composition

1242. 成果/chéng guǒ/ - achievement

1243. 成就/chéng jiù/ - accomplishment

1244. 成语/chéng yǔ/ - idiom; saying; set expression

1245. 成人 /chéng réng/ - adult

1246. 池塘 /chí táng/ - pond

1247. 尺子 /chǐ zi/ - ruler (measuring instrument)

1248. 翅膀 /chì bǎng/ - wing

1249. 充电器 /chōng diàn qì/ - (battery) charger

1250. 宠物 /chǒng wù/ - pet

1251. 抽屉 /chōu ti/ - drawer

1252. 出口 /chū kǒu/ - exit

1253. 除夕 /chú xī/ - Chinese New Year's Eve

1254. 传说 /chuán shuō/ - legend

1255. 传统 /chuán tǒng/ - tradition; traditional

1256. 窗帘 /chuāng lián/ - window curtains

1257. 词汇 /cí huì/ - vocabulary

1258. 醋 /cù/ - vinegar

1259. 措施 /cuò shī/ - measure; step (to be taken)

1260. 大厦 /dà shà/ - mansion

1261. 大象 /dà xiàng/ - elephant

1262. 贷款 /dài kuǎn/ - loan; to loan; to provide a loan

1263. 待遇 /dài yù/ - treatment (in the company)

1264. 单位 /dān wèi/ - unit (to measure); one's workplace

1265. 单元 /dān yuán/ - unit (as an entity)

1266. 胆小鬼 /dǎn xiǎo guǐ/ - coward

1267. 导演 /dǎo yǎn/ - director (film, etc.)

1268. 岛屿 /dǎo yǔ/ - island

1269. 道德 /dào dé/ - morality; ethics; moral

1270. 道理 /dào li/ - reason; logic

她详细说明了这件事的道理。 - She explained the logic behind this issue.

1271. 滴 /dī/ - a drop; to drip

1272. 敌人 /dí rén/ - enemy

1273. 地理/dì lǐ/ - geography

1274. 地区/dì qū/ - area; region; regional

1275. 地毯/dì tǎn/ - carpet

1276. 地位/dì wèi/ - (social, etc.) status; position

1277. 地震/dì zhè/ - earthquake

1278. 点心/diǎn xin/ - pastry; dessert

1279. 电池/diàn chí/ - battery

1280. 电台/diàn tái/ - radio station

1281. 顶/dǐng/ - top; to carry on the head; to push from below or behind; to go against; to retort; to gore; to substitute; to replace; to hold on; measure word for hats, tents, etc.

山顶被积雪覆盖。- The mountaintop was covered with snow.

印度人能用头顶着东西。- Some Indians carry things on their head.

嫩芽把土顶起来了。- The sprouts have pushed up the earth.

我们不得不顶风前进。- We have to go against the wind.

我不想顶你。- I don't want to retort you.

这牛老顶人。- This bull gores people all the time.

患病工人的活儿他顶了。- He substituted for the worker who was ill.

你必须快点来顶我。- You must come quickly to replace me.

你还能再顶一会吗？- Can you hold on a little longer?

1282. 洞/dòng/ - hole

1283. 动画片/dòng huà piàn/ - cartoon

1284. 豆腐/dòu fu/ - tofu; bean curd

1285. 对比/duì bǐ/ - contrast

1286. 对手/duì shǒu/ - opponent

1287. 对象/duì xiàng/ - boyfriend or girlfriend; object; target; partner

这是我对象。- This is my partner.

他成了被嘲弄和鄙视的对象。- He became the object of ridicule and scorn.

他的古怪使他成为他们取笑的对象。- His odd ideas made him the target of their jokes

她到处为儿子物色对象。- She's looking for a suitable partner for her son.

1288. 耳环 /ěr huán/ - earring

1289. 发票 /fā piào/ - invoice

1290. 罚款 /fá kuǎn/ - penalty; fine (monetary)

1291. 法院 /fǎ yuàn/ - court

1292. 方 /fāng/ - Fang (surname)

1293. 方案 /fāng àn/ - plan; proposal

1294. 方式 /fāng shì/ - way (of life); mode

1295. 肥皂 /féi zào/ - soap

1296. 废话 /fèi huà/ - nonsense

1297. 风格 /fēng gé/ - style

1298. 风景 /fēng jǐng/ - scenery; landscape

1299. 风俗 /fēng sú/ - social custom

1300. 风险 /fēng xiǎn/ - risk

1301. 服装 /fú zhuāng/ - clothing; clothes

1302. 妇女 /fù nǚ/ - woman

1303. 盖 /gài/ - lid; to build; to cover

我的杯盖哪去了？- Where is the lid of my cup?

他们在一周内盖起了一家医院。- They managed to build a hospital within a week.

下雨了；找些东西把粮食盖一下。- It's raining; find something to cover the grain.

1304. 概念 /gài niàn/ - concept

1305. 感想 /gǎn xiǎng/ - thoughts; reflections

1306. 钢铁 /gāng tiě/ - steel

1307. 隔壁 /gé bì/ - next door

1308. 个性 /gè xìng/ - personality

1309. 根 /gēn/ - root; measure word for long slender objects, such as cigarettes, chopsticks, etc.

1310. 公寓 /gōng yù/ - apartment; flat

1311. 公元 /gōng yuán/ - (year) AD

1312. 公主 /gōng zhǔ/ - princess

1313. 功能 /gōng néng/ - function

1314. 工厂 /gōng chǎng/ - factory

1315. 工程师 /gōng chéng shī/ - engineer

1316. 工人 /gōng rén/ - worker

1317. 工具 /gōng jù/ - tool

1318. 工业 /gōng yè/ - industry

1319. 姑姑 /gū gu/ - aunt (paternal)

1320. 姑娘 /gū niang/ - girl; young female

1321. 古代 /gǔ dài/ - ancient times

1322. 股票 /gǔ piào/ - stock (market); share

1323. 骨头 /gú tou/ - bone

1324. 官 /guān/ - official; officer

1325. 观点 /guān diǎn/ - viewpoint; opinion

1326. 观念 /guān niàn/ - general impression

1327. 管子 /guǎn zi/ - tube; pipe; drinking straw

1328. 冠军 /guàn jūn/ - champion

1329. 光盘 /guāng pán/ - disc; to clean up the food on the plate

1330. 广场 /guǎng chǎng/ - plaza; a public square

1331. 规矩 /guī ju/ - rule
如果你守规矩，你就不大会遇到麻烦。- If you follow the rules, you are not likely to get into trouble.

1332. 规律 /guī lǜ/ - regular pattern; law (of science, etc.)

1333. 规模 /guī mó/ - scale

1334. 规则/guī zé/ - rule; regulation; prescribed procedure
有规则必有例外。- There are exceptions to the rules.
1335. 柜台/guì tái/ - (sales) counter
1336. 锅/guō/ - wok
1337. 国庆节/guó qìng jié/ - National Day
1338. 国王/guó wáng/ - king
1339. 果实/guǒ shí/ - (ripened) fruit; fruits (of one's labor)
1340. 海关/hǎi guān/ - custom
1341. 海鲜/hǎi xiān/ - seafood
1342. 行业/háng yè/ - business field
1343. 和平/hé píng/ - peace
1344. 合同/hé tong/ - contract
1345. 核心/hé xīn/ - core
1346. 后果/hòu guǒ/ - consequence
1347. 壶/hú/ - pot; measure word for bottled liquid
1348. 蝴蝶/hú dié/ - butterfly
1349. 胡同/hú tong/ - alley
1350. 胡须/hú xū/ - beard
1351. 花生/huā shēng/ - peanut
1352. 滑冰/huá bīng/ - ice skating
1353. 华裔/huá yì/ - ethnic Chinese
1354. 话题/huà tí/ - topic
1355. 化学/huà xué/ - chemistry; chemical
1356. 幻想/huàn xiǎng/ - delusion; fantasy
1357. 黄瓜/huáng guā/ - cucumber
1358. 黄金/huáng jīn/ - gold
1359. 皇帝/huáng dì/ - emperor
1360. 皇后/huáng hòu/ - empress
1361. 灰/huī/ - ash; dust; gray
1362. 灰尘/huī chén/ - dust

1363. 汇率/huì lǜ/ - exchange rate
1364. 婚礼/hūn lǐ/ - wedding
1365. 婚姻/hūn yīn/ - marriage
1366. 火柴/huǒ chái/ - match (for lighting a fire)
1367. 伙伴/huǒ bàn/ - companion
1368. 机器/jī qi/ - machine
1369. 肌肉/jī ròu/ - muscle
1370. 集体/jí tǐ/ - team; collective
这是集体的决定。- It was a collective decision.
我们是一个集体。- We are a team.
1371. 急诊/jí zhěn/ - emergency (medical) treatment
1372. 纪录/jì lù/ - record
该纪录保持了13年，无人能破。- This record figure was unequalled for 13 years.
1373. 纪律/jì lǜ/ - discipline
1374. 记忆/jì yì/ - memory
1375. 嘉宾/jiā bīn/ - esteemed guest; honored guest
1376. 家庭/jiā tíng/ - family
1377. 家务/jiā wù/ - household duties; housework
1378. 家乡/jiā xiāng/ - hometown
1379. 夹子/jiā zi/ - clip; clamp
1380. 假设/jiǎ shè/ - hypothesis; suppose that
1381. 嫁妆/jià zhuang/ - dowry
1382. 价值/jià zhí/ - value; worth
1383. 肩膀/jiān bǎng/ - shoulder
1384. 间距/jiān jù/ - spacing
这是间距问题导致的错误。- This mistake was due to a spacing problem.
1385. 兼职/jiān zhí/ - part time
1386. 简历/jiǎn lì/ - resume

1387. 剪刀/jiǎn dāo/ - scissors
1388. 健身房/jiàn shēn fáng/ - gym
1389. 建筑/jiàn zhù/ - building
1390. 键盘/jiàn pán/ - keyboard
1391. 讲座/jiǎng zuò/ - lecture
1392. 酱油/jiàng yóu/ - soy sauce
1393. 交际/jiāo jì/ - social intercourse.
1394. 郊区/jiāo qū/ - suburban district; outskirts
1395. 胶水/jiāo shuǐ/ - glue
1396. 角度/jiǎo dù/ - angle; point of view
1397. 教材/jiào cái/ - teaching material
1398. 教练/jiào liàn/ - coach
1399. 教训/jiào xun/ - lesson

公司没能从这次经历中吸取任何教训。- The company failed to learn any lessons from this experience.

1400. 阶段/jiē duàn/ - stage; phase

新体系仍处于规划阶段。- The new system is still in the planning stages.

1401. 结构/jié gòu/ - structure
1402. 结论/jié lùn/ - conclusion
1403. 解说员/jiě shuō yuán/ - commentator
1404. 借口/jiè kǒu/ - excuse
1405. 戒指/jiè zhi/ - (finger) ring
1406. 金属/jīn shǔ/ - metal
1407. 近代/jìn dài/ - modern times
1408. 精力/jīng lì/ - vitality; stamina
1409. 景色/jǐng sè/ - scenery; scene; landscape
1410. 酒吧/jiǔ bā/ - pub
1411. 救护车/jiù hù chē/ - ambulance
1412. 舅舅/jiù jiu/ - uncle (mother's brother)

1413. 桔子/jú zǐ/ - tangerine

1414. 聚会/jù huì/ - party; gathering; to get together

1415. 俱乐部/jù lè bù/ - club

1416. 决赛/jué sài/ - finals (of a competition)

1417. 决心/jué xīn/ - determination; to make up one's mind

1418. 角色/jiǎo sè/ - role; character in a novel, play, movie, etc.

1419. 军事/jūn shì/ - military

1420. 卡车/kǎ chē/ - truck

1421. 开幕式/kāi mù shì/ - opening ceremony

1422. 开水/kāi shuǐ/ - boiled water

1423. 烤鸭/kǎo yā/ - roast duck

1424. 课程/kè chéng/ - course

1425. 客厅/kè tīng/ - living room

1426. 空间/kōng jiān/ - space

1427. 口味/kǒu wèi/ - tastes (in food); flavor; a person's preferences

如你所见，这些年来我的口味变了。- My preferences have changed a lot over the years, as you can see.

1428. 会计/kuài jì/ - accountant

1429. 矿泉水/kuàng quán shuǐ/ - mineral water

1430. 昆虫/kūn chóng/ - insect

1431. 辣椒/là jiāo/ - hot pepper; chili

1432. 蜡烛/là zhú/ - candle

1433. 狼/láng/ - wolf

1434. 劳动/láo dòng/ - (physical) labor

1435. 老百姓/lǎo bǎi xìng/ - ordinary people

1436. 老板/lǎo bǎn/ - boss

1437. 老婆/lǎo po/ - wife

1438. 老鼠/lǎo shǔ/ - rat; mouse

1439. 姥姥/lǎo lao/ - grandmother (maternal)

1440. 雷/léi/ - thunder

1441. 类型/lèi xíng/ - type

1442. 梨/lí/ - pear

1443. 理论/lǐ lùn/ - theory

1444. 理由/lǐ yóu/ - reason

1445. 礼拜天/lǐ bài tiān/ - Sunday

1446. 力量/lì liang/ - power; strength

1447. 利润/lì rùn/ - profit

1448. 利息/lì xī/ - interest (on loans or savings)

1449. 利益/lì yì/ - benefit

1450. 连续剧/lián xù jù/ - soap opera

1451. 粮食/liáng shi/ - grain

1452. 列车/liè chē/ - train

1453. 铃/líng/ - bell

1454. 零件/líng jiàn/ - component; part

你们厂有没有这台机器的备用零件？- Does your company have any spare parts for this machine?

1455. 零钱/líng qián/ - change (of money)

1456. 零食/líng shí/ - snack

1457. 领导/lǐng dǎo/ - leader; to lead

我们需要你来领导大家。- We need you to lead us.

1458. 领域/lǐng yù/ - domain

1459. 龙/lóng/ - dragon

1460. 陆地/lù dì/ - dry land

1461. 论文/lùn wén/ - thesis

1462. 逻辑/luó ji/ - logic

1463. 麦克风/mài kè fēng/ - microphone

1464. 馒头/mán tou/ - steamed bun

1465. 毛/máo/ - hair; surname Mao

1466. 毛病/máo bing/ - wrong

你有什么毛病？- What's wrong with you?

1467. 矛盾/máo dùn/ - contradictory

1468. 贸易/mào yì/ - (commercial) trade

1469. 眉毛/méi mao/ - eyebrow

1470. 媒体/méi tǐ/ - media

1471. 煤炭/méi tàn/ - coal

1472. 美术/měi shù/ - art

1473. 魅力/mèi lì/ - charm

1474. 谜语/mí yǔ/ - riddle

1475. 蜜蜂/mì fēng/ - bee

1476. 秘密/mì mì/ - secret

1477. 秘书/mì shū/ - secretary

1478. 棉花/mián hua/ - cotton

1479. 民主/mín zhǔ/ - democracy; democratic

1480. 明信片/míng xìn piàn/ - postcard

1481. 明星/míng xīng/ - celebrity; star (of movie, etc.)

1482. 名牌/míng pái/ - famous brand

1483. 名片/míng piàn/ - name card

1484. 名胜古迹/míng sheng gǔ jì/ - historical sites and scenic spots

1485. 命运/mìng yùn/ - destiny; fate

1486. 摩托车/mó tuō chē/ - motorcycle

1487. 目标/mù biāo/ - target; goal

1488. 目录/mù lù/ - catalog; table of contents

1489. 木头/mù tou/ - wood; blockhead

他简直是个木头，根本不懂得如何表达情感。- He's a blockhead with no idea how to express his feelings.

1490. 脑袋/nǎo dɑi/ - head

1491. 内部/nèi bù/ - inside (part, section); internal

1492. 内科/nèi kē/ - internal medicine

1493. 能源/néng yuán/ - power source

1494. 年代/nián dài/ - era; a decade of a century

1495. 搞年纪/nián jì/ - age

1496. 牛仔裤/niú zī kù/ - jeans

1497. 农民/nóng mín/ - farmer

1498. 农业/nóng yè/ - agriculture

1499. 女士/nǚ shì/ - madam

1500. 排球/pái qiú/ - volleyball

1501. 派/pài/ - pie; to send; to assign

他被派到这儿监视我。- He's been sent here to keep an eye on me.

不久，老板派他到一个新的工作岗位。- Soon, the boss assigned him to a new post.

1502. 盆/pén/ - basin

1503. 拼音/pīn yīn/ - Pinyin

1504. 频道/pín dào/ - channel

1505. 品种/pǐn zhǒng/ - breed

1506. 平衡/píng héng/ - balance

1507. 期间/qī jiān/ - period

1508. 奇迹/qí jì/ - miracle; miraculous

1509. 企业/qǐ yè/ - enterprise

1510. 气氛/qì fēn/ - atmosphere

1511. 汽油/qì yóu/ - gasoline

1512. 前途/qián tú/ - outlook (of the future); vision

1513. 枪/qiāng/ - gun

1514. 墙/qiáng/ - wall

1515. 青春/qīng chūn/ - youth

1516. 青少年/qīng shào nián/ - youngster

1517. 情景/qíng jǐng/ - scene

1518. 情绪/qíng xù/ - feeling

1519. 趋势 /qū shì/ - trend

1520. 权力 /quán lì/ - authority; power

在民主政体中，权力必须分制。- In a democracy, power must be divided.

只有经理才有权力签支票。- Only the manager has the authority to sign checks.

1521. 权利 /quán lì/ - privilege; right

在我国女性享有同男性一样的权利。- Women in our country enjoy equal rights with men.

他显然滥用了这项权利。- He's obviously abusing the privilege.

Chapter 7 Nouns (R ~ Z)

1522. 人才/rén cái/ - talented person
1523. 人口/rén kǒu/ - population
1524. 人类/rén lèi/ - humanity; human race; mankind
1525. 人生/rén shēng/ - (human) life
1526. 人事/rén shì/ - human resources
1527. 人物/rén wù/ - character (in a movie or book)
1528. 人员/rén yuán/ - personnel
1529. 日程/rì chéng/ - schedule; itinerary
1530. 日历/rì lì/ - calendar
1531. 日期/rì qī/ - date
1532. 日用品/rì yòng pǐn/ - everyday items
1533. 荣誉/róng yù/ - honor
她用荣誉换取财富。- She exchanged honor for wealth.
1534. 嗓子/sǎng zi/ - throat; voice
我嗓子疼。- I have a sore throat.
她有副嗓子。- She has a beautiful voice.
1535. 沙漠/shā mò/ - desert
1536. 沙滩/shā tān/ - beach

1537. 闪电 /shǎn diàn/ - lightning

1538. 扇子 /shàn zi/ - fan

我们的扇子分三大类：纸扇，绸扇和檀香木扇。- We have three major types of fan: paper, silk, and sandalwood.

1539. 商品 /shāng pǐn/ - commodity; merchandise

1540. 商业 /shāng yè/ - commerce

1541. 勺子 /sháo zi/ - spoon; ladle; scoop

1542. 蛇 /shé/ - snake

1543. 舌头 /shé tou/ - tongue

1544. 设备 /shè bèi/ - equipment; facility

增加了生产设备后，我们要做广告争取更多客户。- Having increased our manufacturing capabilities, we've begun advertising to obtain more clients.

他们公司提供厨房设备。- Their company supplies kitchen equipment.

1545. 设施 /shè shī/ - facility; installation

我们城市需要更多的娱乐设施。- Our city needs more amusement facilities.

该建筑被改造成了一处秘密军事设施。- The building was turned into a secret military installation.

1546. 摄影 /shè yǐng/ - photography

1547. 身材 /shēn cái/ - build (height and weight)

1548. 身份 /shēn fèn/ - identity; dignity

他并不认为这么做有失身份。- He did not consider it's beneath his dignity to do these things.

1549. 神话 /shén huà/ - fairy tale

1550. 神经 /shén jīng/ - nerve

1551. 声调 /shēng diào/ - tone

1552. 绳子 /shéng zi/ - rope

1553. 胜利 /shèng lì/ - victory

1554. 诗 /shī/ - poem

1555. 失眠 /shī mián/ - insomnia

1556. 时代 /shí dài/ - era

1557. 时刻 /shí kè/ - moment; always

正是这些开心的时刻让生活有了意义。- Those are the happy moments which make life worth living.

敌人时刻都在谋划着。- The enemy is always scheming and plotting.

1558. 时期 /shí qī/ - a period in time or history

1559. 实话 /shí huà/ - truth

快说实话！- Tell the truth!

1560. 实习 /shí xí/ - internship

1561. 食物 /shí wù/ - food

1562. 石头 /shí tou/ - stone

1563. 试卷 /shì juàn/ - test paper

1564. 士兵 /shì bīng/ - soldier

1565. 事实 /shì shí/ - fact

1566. 事物 /shì wù/ - thing

他们可以参观许多地方并且看到许多事物。- They can visit many places and see many things.

1567. 收获 /shōu huò/ - harvest

1568. 收据 /shōu jù/ - receipt

1569. 手术 /shǒu shù/ - surgery

1570. 手套 /shǒu tào/ - glove; mitten

1571. 手续 /shǒu xù/ - formality

1572. 手指 /shǒu zhǐ/ - finger

1573. 寿命 /shòu mìng/ - life expectancy

1574. 书架 /shū jià/ - bookshelf

1575. 蔬菜 /shū cài/ - vegetable

1576. 梳子 /shū zi/ - comb

1577. 鼠标 /shǔ biāo/ - mouse (computing)

1578. 数据/shù jù/ – data

1579. 税/shuì/ – tax

1580. 丝绸/sī chóu/ – silk

1581. 思想/sī xiǎng/ – thinking

1582. 寺庙/sì miào/ – temple

1583. 宿舍/sù shè/ – dormitory

1584. 损失/sǔn shī/ – loss; to lose

1585. 塔/tǎ/ – tower

1586. 台阶/tái jiē/ – step (over obstacle)

1587. 太极拳/tài jí quán/ – Tai Chi

1588. 太太/tài tai/ – Mrs.

1589. 桃/táo/ – peach

1590. 特征/tè zhēng/ – distinctive feather

1591. 提纲/tí gāng/ – outline

1592. 题目/tí mù/ – subject; topic

我对这个题目没兴趣。– I'm not interested in this subject.

他买了许多与此题目有关的书。– He bought many books relating to this topic.

1593. 体积/tǐ jī/ – volume

1594. 天空/tiān kōng/ – sky

1595. 田野/tián yě/ – field

这是一种田野里常见的花。– It's a flower common in the field.

1596. 通讯/tōng xùn/ – communication

他们的通讯系统效率低下。– Their communications systems are extremely inefficient.

1597. 铜/tóng/ – copper

1598. 土地/tǔ dì/ – land

1599. 土豆/tǔ dòu/ – potato

1600. 兔子/tù zǐ/ – rabbit

1601. 优势/yōu shì/ – advantage; superiority

1602. 外公/wài gōng/ - grandfather (maternal)

1603. 外交/wài jiāo/ - diplomacy; diplomatic

1604. 玩具/wán jù/ - toy

1605. 王子/wáng zǐ/ - prince

1606. 网络/wǎng luò/ - network

1607. 微笑/wēi xiào/ - smile

1608. 围巾/wéi jīn/ - scarf

1609. 尾巴/wěi ba/ - tail

1610. 胃/wèi/ - stomach

1611. 胃口/wèi kǒu/ - appetite

1612. 位置/wèi zhi/ - location

1613. 未来/wèi lái/ - future

1614. 卫生间/wèi shēng jiān/ - bathroom; toilet

1615. 文件/wén jiàn/ - document; file

1616. 文具/wén jù/ - stationery

1617. 文学/wén xué/ - literature

1618. 吻/wěn/ - kiss; to kiss

1619. 卧室/wò shì/ - bedroom

1620. 屋子/wū zi/ - house

1621. 武器/wǔ qì/ - weapon

1622. 武术/wǔ shù/ - martial art

1623. 雾/wù/ - fog; mist

1624. 物理/wù lǐ/ - physics; physical

1625. 物质/wù zhì/ - matter; substance
他专门研究暗物质。- He specializes in dark matter.

1626. 系统/xì tǒng/ - system

1627. 细节/xì jié/ - detail

1628. 戏剧/xì jù/ - drama

1629. 夏令营/xià lìng yíng/ - summer camp

1630. 县/xiàn/ - county

1631. 现金/xiàn jīn/ - cash

1632. 现象/xiàn xiàng/ - phenomenon

1633. 香肠/xiāng cháng/ - sausage

1634. 项链/xiàng liàn/ - necklace

1635. 项目/xiàng mù/ - project

1636. 橡皮/xiàng pí/ - eraser

1637. 象棋/xiàng qí/ - Chinese Chess

1638. 小吃/xiǎo chī/ - snack

1639. 小伙子/xiǎo huǒ zi/ - young man

1640. 小麦/xiǎo mài/ - wheat

1641. 小偷/xiǎo tōu/ - thief

1642. 效率/xiào lǜ/ - efficiency

1643. 心理/xīn lǐ/ - mental; psychological

1644. 心脏/xīn zàng/ - heart

1645. 信封/xìn fēng/ - envelop

1646. 信号/xìn hào/ - signal

1647. 信息/xìn xī/ - information; news; message

1648 行动/xíng dòng/ - action; to more

1649. 行人/xíng rén/ - pedestrian

1650. 行为/xíng wéi/ - behavior

1651. 形式/xíng shì/ - form

我反对任何形式地狩猎。- I am against hunting in any form.

1652. 形势/xíng shì/ - situation

他非常周密地分析了形势。- He analyzed the situation very deeply.

1653. 形状/xíng zhuàng/ - shape

1654. 性质/xìng zhì/ - nature

他对自己使命的确切性质还不清楚。- He was not clear on the precise nature of his mission.

1655. 胸/xiōng/ - chest

1656. 兄弟/xiōng di/ - dude

1657. 休闲/xiū xián/ - leisure

1658. 学历/xué lì/ - educational background

1659. 学期/xué qī/ - semester

1660. 学术/xué shù/ - academic

1661. 血/xiě/ - blood

1662. 演讲/yǎn jiǎng/ - lecture

1663. 宴会/yàn huì/ - banquet

1664. 阳台/yáng tái/ - balcony; porch

1665. 样式/yàng shì/ - style

1666. 腰/yāo/ - waist

1667. 夜/yè/ - night

冬天昼短夜长。- In winter the days are short and the nights long.

1668. 液体/yè tǐ/ - liquid

1669. 业务/yè wù/ - business; vocational work

我有一家药店,想要扩大业务。- I owned a drugstore and wanted to expand the business.

管理咨询是我公司的一项核心业务。- Management consulting is a major vocation in the company.

1670. 一辈子/yí bèi zi/ - for a lifetime

1671. 疑问/yí wèn/ - question; doubt

1672. 意见/yì jian/ - opinion; suggestion

1673. 意外/yì wài/ - accident; unforeseen

他死于一场意外。- He died in an accident.

这是她好运中的一次意外挫折。- It was an unforeseen setback in her fortunes.

1674. 意义/yì yi/ - meaning

1675. 义务/yì wù/ - obligation

1676. 因素/yīn sù/ - factor

1677. 银/yín/ - silver

1678. 英雄 /yīng xióng/ - hero
1679. 营养 /yíng yǎng/ - nutrition; nourishment
1680. 影子 /yǐng zi/ - shadow
1681. 硬币 /yìng bì/ - coin
1682. 硬件 /yìng jiàn/ - hardware
1683. 勇气 /yǒng qì/ - courage
1684. 用途 /yòng tú/ - purpose
他坚称这笔捐款将用于国际用途。- He has maintained that the money was donated for international purposes.
1685. 邮局 /yóu jú/ - post office
1686. 幼儿园 /yòu ér yuán/ - kindergarten
1687. 语气 /yǔ qì/ - tone (of speech)
医生的语气很严肃。- The doctor's tone was serious.
1688. 宇宙 /yǔ zhòu/ - universe
1689. 预报 /yù bào/ - forecast; to forecast
1690. 玉米 /yù mǐ/ - corn
1691. 元旦 /yuán dàn/ - New Year's Day
1692. 缘故 /yuán gù/ - reason
1693. 原料 /yuán liào/ - raw material
1694. 原则 /yuán zé/ - in principle
1695. 员工 /yuán gōng/ - employee
1696. 愿望 /yuàn wàng/ - wish
1697. 乐器 /yuè qì/ - musical instrument
1698. 运气 /yùn qi/ - luck
1699. 灾害 /zāi hài/ - disaster
1700. 战争 /zhàn zhēng/ - war
1701. 长辈 /zhǎng bèi/ - one's elders
1702. 账户 /zhàng hù/ - account
1703. 哲学 /zhé xué/ - philosophy
1704. 真理 /zhēn lǐ/ - truth

真理面前，人人平等。- Everyone is equal before the truth.

1705. 枕头/zhěn tou/ - pillow

1706. 整体/zhěng tǐ/ - whole

城市规划将城市视为一个有机的整体。- Urban planning treats the city as an organic whole.

1707. 政府/zhèng fǔ/ - government

1708. 政治/zhèng zhì/ - politics; political

1709. 证件/zhèng jiàn/ - credentials

1710. 证据/zhèng jù/ - evidence; proof

1711. 支票/zhī piào/ - check

1712. 执照/zhí zhào/ - license

1713. 制度/zhì dù/ - (political, administrative, etc.) system

1714. 智慧/zhì huì/ - wisdom

1715. 秩序/zhì xù/ - order

旧的社会秩序一去不复返。- The old social order was gone forever.

警察是法律和秩序地守护者。- The police are guardians of law and order.

1716. 志愿者/zhì yuàn zhě/ - volunteer

1717. 钟/zhōng/ - clock; Zhong (surname)

1718. 中介/zhōng jiè/ - agency; mediation

我们得通过中介雇佣保姆。- We had to hire a nanny through an agency.

该应用提供了位置、协议和一系列中介功能。- The application provides location, protocol, and a number of mediation capabilities.

1719. 中心/zhōng xīn/ - center

1720. 中旬/zhōng xún/ - middle of a month

1721. 种类/zhǒng lèi/ - type

1722. 重量/zhòng liàng/ - weight

1723. 竹子/zhú zǐ/ - bamboo

1724. 主人/zhǔ rén/ - host; hostess; master

旧社会的奴隶变成了新社会的主人。- The slaves of the old society have become the masters of the new society.

1725. 主任/zhǔ rèng/ - director; head (of an office, etc.)

1726. 主题/zhǔ tí/ - theme

1727. 主席/zhǔ xí/ - chairperson

1728. 主张/zhǔ zhāng/ - proposal; advocacy; to stand for

两种主张都有道理。- Both proposals sound reasonable.

我支持你自由贸易的主张。- I support your advocacy of free trade.

他主张将国家从教条的控制下解放出来。- He stands for freeing the country from the grip of dogma.

1729. 专家/zhuān jiā/ - expert

1730. 资格/zī ge/ - qualification

1731. 资金/zī jīn/ - funds; funding

1732. 资源/zī yuán/ - resource

1733. 姿势/zī shì/ - posture

1734. 字母/zì mǔ/ - letter (of the alphabet)

1735. 字幕/zì mù/ - subtitle

1736. 自信/zì xìn/ - self-confidence

1737. 自由/zì yóu/ - freedom; liberty

1738. 宗教/zōng jiào/ - religion

1739. 总裁/zǒng cái/ - CEO

1740. 总理/zǒng lǐ/ - premier; prime minister

1741. 总统/zǒng tǒng/ - president (of a country)

1742. 祖国/zǔ guó/ - homeland

1743. 祖先/zǔ xiān/ - ancestor

1744. 罪犯/zuì fàn/ - criminals

1745. 作品/zuò pǐn/ - work (of art, literature, etc.)

1746. 作文/zuò wén/ – composition (student essay)

Chapter 8. Verbs (A ~ L)

1747. 爱护/ài hù/ - to take care of; to cherish; to love and to protect

1748. 爱惜/ài xī/ - to cherish; to use sparingly

1749. 安慰/ān wèi/ - to comfort

1750. 安装/ān zhuāng/ - to install

1751. 熬夜/áo yè/ - to stay up late

1752. 把握/bǎ wò/ - to grasp; to seize; sure (of the outcome)

你一定要把握住这次机会。- You really need to grasp this opportunity.

我可没有把握做这件事。- I'm not sure about doing this.

1753. 摆/bǎi/ - to arrange; to put

1754. 办理/bàn lǐ/ - to handle; to deal with; to conduct

1755. 包含/bāo hán/ - to contain; to include

1756. 保持/bǎo chí/ - to keep; to maintain; to hold

几年来,我和她一直保持联系。- I kept in touch with her for several years.

该部门与化工行业保持着众多密切的联系。- The department maintains many close contacts with the chemical industry.

这样的好天气能保持多久？- How long will the fine weather hold?

1757. 保存/bǎo cún/ - to preserve; to keep; to save (computing)
这些书保存得很好。- These books are well preserved.
校长把我校的所有报告都存档保存。- The principal keeps all our school reports on file.
从扫描仪导入扫描后的图像，并保存为JPG文件。- Import your images from the scanner and save them as JPG files.

1758. 保留/bǎo liú/ - to retain; to preserve; to reserve
他还保留着战争年代的革命朝气。- He still retains the revolutionary fervor of the war years.
她保留了改变主意的权利。- She reserved the right to change her mind.
市政府花了不少钱来保留那座古堡。- The city government spent a lot of money to preserve the old castle.

1759. 报到/bào dào/ - to report for duty; to check in

1760. 抱怨/bào yuàn/ - to complain; complaint

1761. 背/bēi/ - to give a piggyback
/bèi/ - to recite; the back of a body or object; to turn one's back

1762. 避免/bì miǎn/ - to avoid

1763. 编辑/biān ji/ - to edit; editor

1764. 辩论/biàn lùn/ - to argue over; debate

1765. 表明/biǎo míng/ - to make clear; to indicate
我们今天的投票表明了政策得一种变化。- Our vote today indicates a change in policy.

1766. 表现/biǎo xiàn/ - to show; behavior (at school); performance (at work)
他在逆境中表现出了勇气。- He showed courage in adversity.
她因在校表现好而获奖。- She won a prize for good behavior at school.

1767. 播放/bō fàng/ - to broadcast

1768. 补充 /bǔ chōng/ - to replenish; supplementary

1769. 踩 /cǎi/ - to step on

1770. 采访 /cǎi fǎng/ - to interview

1771. 采取 /cǎi qǔ/ - to adopt or carry out (measures, policies, course of action)

1772. 参与 /cān yù/ - to participate

1773. 操心 /cāo xīn/ - to worry about

1774. 测验 /cè yàn/ - to test; test

1775. 产生 /chǎn shēng/ - to come into being; to emerge

第一个工人联盟就这样产生了。- Thus, the first worker's league came into being.

你们的会谈产生了什么结果？- What was the result of your discussion?

1776. 炒 /chǎo/ - to stir-fry; to fire

他被炒了。- He was fired.

1777. 吵架 /chǎo jià/ - to quarrel

1778. 趁 /chèn/ - to take (advantage of); (while)

我想趁这个机会讲几句话。- I'd like to take this opportunity to say a few words.

这面得趁热吃。- Eat the noodles while they are still hot.

1779. 称 /chēng/ - to weigh; to name

我们都称他铁牛。- We all call him iron ox.

1780. 称呼 /chēng hu/ - to name; appellation

他被称呼为先驱。- He was called a pioneer.

他赢得了"反叛牧师"的称呼。- He earned the appellation "rebel priest".

1781. 称赞 /chēng zàn/ - to praise; to compliment

1782. 承担 /chéng dān/ - to undertake: to assume (responsibility, etc.)

1783. 承认 /chéng rèn/ - to admit

1784. 承受/chéng shòu/ - to bear

1785. 成立/chéng lì/ - to establish; to set up

1786. 成长/chéng zhǎng/ - to grow; growth

1787. 吃亏/chī kuī/ - to be at a disadvantage; to lose out; to suffer losses

跟他做生意你是要吃亏的。- You'll suffer losses if you do business with him.

在新一轮的薪资弹性化政策中吃亏的是女性。- Women have lost out in this new pay flexibility scheme.

1788. 充满/chōng mǎn/ - to be full of; to be brimming with; to be filled with

他充满了悔恨。- He was filled with remorse.

这本书里充满了真实有趣的人物形象。- This book is full of believable interesting characters.

她两眼充满泪水。- Her eyes were brimming with tears.

1789. 重复/chóng fù/ - to repeat; to duplicate

1790. 出版/chū bǎn/ - to publish

1791. 出示/chū shì/ - to (take out and) show

请出示护照。- Please show me your passport.

1792. 出席/chū xí/ - to attend

1793. 处理/chǔ lǐ/ - to process

1794. 传播/chuán bō/ - to spread; to propagate

1795. 传染/chuán rǎn/ - to infect; contagious

1796. 闯/chuǎng/ - to break through; to temper oneself (through battling hardships)

1797. 创造/chuàng zào/ - to create; to innovate

1798. 吹/chuī/ - to blow; to bring; to play (a wind instrument); to puff; to brag; to fall through

那个男孩在吹泡泡。- The boy over there was blowing bubbles.

什么风把你吹来了？ - What brings you here?

她长笛吹得不错。- She plays the flute quite well.

先别吹；做出具体成绩来再说。- Don't brag about what you're going to do; get something done first.

他们把他吹上了天。- They talked him up (to the skies).

原来的计划吹了。- The original plan has fallen through.

1799. 辞职/cí zhí/ - to resign

1800. 刺激/cì jī/ - to stimulate; to provoke; to irritate

1801. 从事/cóng shì / - to engage in; to undertake

1802. 促进/cù jìn/ - to promote; to boost

体育活动促进身体健康。- Physical activity promotes good health.

出口产业将促进经济发展。- The export sector will boost the economy.

1803. 促使/cù shǐ/ - to impel; to drive (someone to do something)

生产的发展促使我们不断钻研技术。- The development of production impels us continuously to study new techniques.

那么是什么促使他这么做的呢？- What drove him to do something like this?

1804. 催/cuī/ - to rush someone

1805. 存在/cún zài/ - to exist

1806. 答应/dā ying/ - to agree

1807. 达到/dá dào/ - to achieve; to attain

1808. 打工/dǎ gōng/ - to work

1809. 打交道/dǎ jiāo dào/ - to have dealings with; to deal with

不要和那个人打交道。- Don't have any dealings with that fellow.

我们经常跟他打交道。- We often deal with him.

1810. 打喷嚏/dǎ pēn tì/ - to sneeze

1811. 打听/dǎ ting/ - to ask about; to inquire about

我想跟你打听个事。- I'd like to ask you about something.

他到医院去打听她的情况。- He went to the hospital to inquire about her.

1812. 呆/dāi/ - to stay; stupid
医生劝我在家呆几天。- The doctor advised me to stay in for a few days.
他是个呆子。- He's a stupid guy.

1813. 担任/dān rèn/ - to serve as; to hold a post

1814. 耽误/ dān wu/ - to delay; to waste time; to interfere with

1815. 当心/dāng xīn/ - to look out

1816. 挡/dǎng/ - to block; to hold; to stand in the way; gear
一条大河挡住了前路。- A big river blocks the way.
叫那个男孩别挡道。- Tell the boy not to stand in the way.
在山上，他得挂低速挡。- On hills, he must use low gears.
我们的军队快挡不住敌人了。- Our army can't hold back the enemy.

1817. 倒霉/dǎo méi/ - to have bad luck

1818. 导致/dǎo zhì/ - to lead to; to cause

1819. 到达/dào dá/ - to arrive

1820. 登记/dēng jì/ - to register

1821. 等待/děng dài/ - to wait for

1822. 等于/děng yú/ - to equal to

1823. 递/dì/ - to hand over; to pass on something; progressively
该委员会从政府处获得的津贴年年递减。- The grants the council received from the government was progressively reduced every year.

1824. 钓/diào/ - to fish

1825. 冻/dòng/ - to freeze

1826. 逗/dòu/ - to tease

1827. 度过/dù guò/ - to spend (time); to get through; to survive
我相信你能度过难关。- I believe you can survive this.

1828. 堆/duī/ - to pile up; pile (of things)

1829. 兑换/duì huàn/ - to convert; to exchange

1830. 对待/duì dài/ - to treat; treatment

1831. 蹲/dūn/ - to crouch

1832. 顿/dùn/ - to pause; pause; measure word for meals, beating, telling off, etc.

在讲这件事时，她顿了好几下。 - While talking about it, she paused several times.

他顿了一顿，又接着说下去。 - After a short pause, he went on.

1833. 躲藏/duǒ cáng/ - to hide

1834. 发表/fā biǎo/ - to publish; to issue (a statement)

我把他的草稿重新改写，并以我的名义发表了。 - I rewrote his draft and published it under my name.

他发表了一个简短隐晦的声明，否认对其间谍行为的指控。 - He has issued a short, cryptic statement denying the espionage charges.

1835. 发愁/fā chóu/ - to be anxious; to worry; to become sad

1836. 发抖/fā dǒu/ - to tremble

1837. 发挥/fā huī/ - to bring into play

发挥中央和地方两个积极性。 - Both central and local initiatives should be brought into play.

1838. 发明/fā míng/ - to invent; invention

1839. 发言/fā yán/ - to make a speech; statement

1840. 翻/fān/ - to turn over; to flip over

1841. 反应/fǎn yìng/ - to react; reaction

1842. 妨碍/fáng ài/ - to hinder; to obstruct

1843. 分别/fēn bié/ - to part; to distinguish; difference; separately

他们已分别多年了。 - They were parted for years.

你必须学会分别善恶。 - You must learn to distinguish good from evil.

两者之间没有任何分别。 - There is no difference between the two.

我需要分别和他们谈谈。 - I need to talk with them separately.

1844. 分布 /fēn bù/ – to distribute
1845. 分配 /fēn pèi/ – to allocate; to assign
1846. 分手 /fēn shǒu/ – to break up
1847. 分析 /fēn xī/ – to analyze; analysis
1848. 奋斗 /fèn dòu/ – to strive
1849. 讽刺 /fěng cì/ – to satirize; sarcasm; irony
1850. 否定 /fǒu dìng/ – to negate; negative (answer)
1851. 否认 /fǒu rèn/ – to deny
1852. 扶 /fú/ – to support with hand
1853. 辅导 /fǔ dǎo/ – to coach; to give advice (in study)
1854. 复制 /fù zhì/ – to copy; to duplicate
1855. 改革 /gǎi gé/ – to reform; reform
1856. 改进 /gǎi jìn/ – to improve; improvement

教师们如何才能改进教学以激发创造性呢？– How can faculty improve their teaching to encourage creativity?

还有改进的余地。– There is still room for improvement.

1857. 改善 /gǎi shàn/ – to improve; to make better

必须兼顾发展生产和改善生活。– Consideration must be given to both the development of production and the improvement of livelihoods.

两国关系已有所改善。– The relations between the two countries have shown some improvement.

1858. 改正 /gǎi zhèng/ – to correct; correction
1859. 概括 /gài kuò/ – to summarize; to generalize
1860. 感激 /gǎn jī/ – to express thanks; grateful
1861. 感受 /gǎn shòu/ – to sense; to feel; perception
1862. 赶紧 /gǎn jǐn/ – to hurry up; hurriedly
1863. 干活儿 /gàn huór/ – to get to work

1864. 搞/gǎo/ - to do; to carry on; to be engaged in; to work out; to produce; to play (tricks, plots, etc.); to set up; to make (food, money, etc.); to get hold of

你脸上怎么搞的？- What have you done to your face?

中国一直在搞计划生育。- China has carried out birth control for quite a long time.

她丈夫是搞科学研究的。- Her husband is engaged in scientific research.

图纸搞出来了吗？- Has the drawing been worked out?

我们也可以搞一些这样的产品。- We can also produce something like this.

别跟我搞花样！- Don't play tricks on me!

当地政府打算在这里搞一个工业园。- The local government is thinking of setting up an industrial zone here.

这些人只想搞钱。- These people are just interested in making money.

我搞到两张音乐会的票。- I've got hold of two tickets for the concert.

1865. 告别/gào bié/ - to say goodbye

1866. 公布/gōng bù/ - to announce

政府已经公布了一系列帮助电影业的措施。- The government has announced a package of measures to help the film industry.

1867. 贡献/gòng xiàn/ - to contribute; contribution

1868. 沟通/gōu tōng/ - to communicate; communication

1869. 构成/gòu chéng/ - to constitute; to compose

1870. 鼓舞/gǔ wǔ/ - to boost (morale)

1871. 挂号/guà hào/ - to register (at a hospital)

1872. 拐弯/guǎi wān/ - to turn a corner

1873. 关闭/guān bì/ - to close; to shut

1874. 观察/guān chá/ - to observe; observation

1875. 光临/guāng lín/ - (it is an honor to) have you here

1876. 归纳/guī nà/ - to sum up; to conclude

1877. 滚/gǔn/ - to roll; to get lost (imperative)

1878. 过敏/guò mǐn/ - to be allergic; allergy

1879. 过期/guò qī/ - to expire; expiration

1880. 哈/hā/ - to blow one's breath; ha (laughter); aha
他在窗户玻璃上哈了一口气。- He blew a breath of air on a windowpane.

1881. 喊/hǎn/ - to shout; to yell

1882. 合谋/hé móu/ - to plan something together

1883. 合影/hé yǐng/ - to have a group photo taken

1884. 合作/hé zuò/ - to cooperate; to collaborate; cooperation

1885. 恨/hèn/ - to hate; to regret; hate
她恨你就因为你说的那句话。- She hates you for saying that.
我恨自己结婚太早。- I regret that I got married so young.
爱与恨可以共存吗？- Can love and hate coexist?

1886. 忽视/hū shì/ - to neglect; to ignore

1887. 呼吸/hū xī/ - to breathe

1888. 胡说/hú shuō/ - to talk nonsense

1889. 糊涂/hú tu/ - to be confused; muddled

1890. 划船/huá chuán/ - to paddle a boat

1891. 滑/huá/ - to slip; to slide; slippery

1892. 怀念/huái niàn/ - to cherish the memory of

1893. 缓解/huǎn jiě/ - to ease; to help relieve

1894. 挥/huī/ - to wave

1895. 挥别/huī bié/ - to wave goodbye

1896. 灰心/huī xīn/ - to be discouraged; to lose heart
别灰心！- Don't be discouraged! (Don't lose heart!)

1897. 恢复/huī fù/ - to resume; to recover; to regain; to restore
预期很快能恢复交通。- Traffic is expected to resume shortly.

我恢复了健康，并娶了那所医院一位护理我的护士。- I recovered and married one of my nurses from the hospital.

我拼命恢复自己的一点儿尊严。- I struggled to regain some dignity.

这座城市终于恢复了平静。- Peace was finally restored to the city.

1898. 回收/huí shōu/ - to recycle

1899. 回首/huí shǒu/ - to look back (on the past)

1900. 及格/jí gé/ - to pass a test

1901. 集中/jí zhōng/ - to concentrate; to focus; concentration

工业区集中在东部和西部。- The industrial districts are concentrated in the east and the west.

现在投票更趋集中了。- Voting is now more focused.

我们注意力不够集中，结果丢了球，输了比赛。- We lacked concentration, and it cost us the goal and the game.

1902. 系领带/jì lǐng dài/ - to tie one's necktie

1903. 记录/jì lù/ - to take notes; record

他的发言我都记录下来了。- I've taken notes on what he said.

对他的指控包括诈骗、行贿和伪造商业记录。- The charges against him include fraud, bribery, and falsifying business records.

1905. 纪念/jì niàn/ - to commemorate; to remember; commemorative

政府要为纪念战争死难者的举行教堂礼拜仪式。- The government is going to provide a church service to remember those who died in the war.

1906. 计算/jì suàn/ - to calculate

1907. 假装/jiǎ zhuāng/ - to pretend

1908. 嫁/jià/ - (of a woman) to marry; to marry (off a daughter)

1909. 嫁祸/jià huò/ - to shift the blame onto someone else; to frame

1910. 驾驶/jià shǐ/ - to drive (a vehicle); to pilot (a ship, a plane, etc.)

1911. 煎/jiān/ - to fry

1912. 捡/jiǎn/ - to pick up (from the ground)

1913. 健身/jiàn shēn/ - to exercise; to keep fit; to work out

1914. 建立/jiàn lì/ - to establish; to found

1915. 建设/jiàn shè/ - to construct

1916. 讲究/jiǎng jiu/ - to be fastidious about; to pay attention to
她非常讲究仪表。- She was fastidious about her appearance.
他不怎么讲究吃喝。- He doesn't pay attention to what he eats or drinks.

1917. 浇/jiāo/ - to water; to cast (molten metal); to pour liquid

1918. 交换/jiāo huàn/ - to exchange; to switch

1919. 交往/jiāo wǎng/ - to associate; to go out with; to date

1920. 接触/jiē chù/ - to contact; to touch; in touch with

1921. 接待/jiē dài/ - to receive (a visitor or a guest)

1922. 接近/jiē jìn/ - to approach someone; close to; near

1923. 接吻/jiē wěn/ - to kiss each other on the lips

1924. 接着/jiē zhe/ - to catch and hold on; to go on to do something; then; after that

1925. 节省/jié shěng/ - to save (resources, money, etc.); to cut down on

1926. 结合/jié hé/ - to combine

1927. 结算/jié suàn/ - to settle accounts; to balance accounts

1928. 结账/jié zhàng/ - to pay the bill

1929. 解放/jiě fàng/ - to emancipate; to liberate

1930. 戒/jiè/ - to give up or stop doing something

1931. 戒烟/jiè yān/ - to quit smoking

1932. 进步/jìn bù/ - to progress

1933. 进口/jìn kǒu/ - to import; imported; inlet

1934. 尽力/jìn lì/ - to spare no effort;

1935. 经商/jīng shāng/ - to be in business

1936. 经营/jīng yíng/ - to engage in (business, etc.); to operate (a store, etc.)

1937. 救/jiù/ - to rescue; to save

1938. 具备/jù bèi/ - to possess (conditions or requirements)

1939. 捐/juān/ - to donate

1940. 开发/kāi fā/ - to develop

1941. 开放/kāi fàng/ - to open to the outside world; to open (for public): to come into bloom (of flowers)

中国要进一步扩大开放范围。- China will further expand the scope of its opened-up areas.

该旅馆已向客人开放。- The hotel is now open to guests.

玫瑰花已经开放。- The roses have come into bloom.

1942. 开心/kāi xīn/ - to have a great time; to feel happy

1943. 砍/kǎn/ - to chop; to cut down

1944. 看不起/kàn bu qǐ/ - to look down upon

1945. 看望/kàn wàng/ - to pay a call to

1946. 抗议/kàng yì/ - to protest

1947. 克服/kè fú/ - to overcome

1948. 刻苦/kè kǔ/ - to study hard

他从此将会刻苦学习。- He will study harder from now on.

1949. 控制/kòng zhì/ - to control

1950. 夸张/kuā zhāng/ - to exaggerate; exaggerated

1951. 来自/lái zì/ - to come from

1952. 朗读/lǎng dú/ - to read aloud

1953. 劳驾/láo jià/ - excuse me

1954. 离婚/lí hūn/ - to divorce

1955. 利用/lì yòng/ - to make use of; to take advantage of

1956. 联合/lián hé/ - to make an alliance; to unite

1957. 恋爱/liàn ài/ - to be in love

1958. 流传/liú chuán/ - to spread

1959. 浏览/liú lǎn/ - to browse; to skim over

1960. 漏/lòu/ - to leak; to leave out (by mistake)

水从管子中漏出。- The water leaked from the pipe.

印刷工人把这一段漏了两行。- The printer has left out two lines from this paragraph.

1961. 录取/lù qǔ/ - to enroll

1962. 录音/lù yīn/ - to record (sound); sound recording

1963. 轮流/lún liú/ - to take turns

1964. 落后/luò hòu/ - to fall behind

Chapter 9 Verbs (M ~ Z)

1965. 骂/mà/ - to scold; abuse

1966. 满足/mǎn zú/ - to satisfy; to meet (the needs of); to be satisfied

为了满足好奇心，我们去了鬼屋。- To satisfy our own curiosity, we went into the haunted house.

我们可以满足你的一切需要。- We can meet all your needs.

他对自己的所得从不感到满足。- He's never satisfied with what he's got.

1967. 冒险/mào xiǎn/ - to take risks; to take chances; adventure

1968. 迷路/mí lù/ - to be lost; to lose the way

1969. 面对/miàn duì/ - to face; to confront

面对证据，他承认有罪。- Faced with the evidence, he admitted his guilt.

我们必须乐观面对未来。- We must face the future with optimism.

1970. 面临/miàn lín/ - to be confronted

她面临严峻的资金问题。- She was confronted with severe financial problems.

1971. 描写/miáo xiě/ - to describe (with writing); description (on paper)

1972. 明确/míng què/ - to clarify; to specify

1973. 命令/mìng lìng/ - to command; command

1974. 模仿/mó fǎng/ - to imitate; to mimic

1975. 念/niàn/ - to read

1976. 拍/pāi/ - to pat; to flap; to take (a photo); to clap; to shoot (a movie)

我拍了拍小狗的头。- I patted the puppy on the head.

她用报纸拍苍蝇。- She smacked the newspaper at the fly.

能和我拍张照吗？- Can you take a photo with me?

他高兴地拍起手来。- He clapped her hands in delight.

这部电影是在澳大利亚拍的。- This film was shot in Australia.

1977. 排队/pái duì/ - to line up; to form a line

1978. 盼望/pàn wàng/ - to hope for; to look forward to

1979. 赔偿/péi cháng/ - to compensate

1980. 培养/péi yǎng/ - to breed

1981. 培训/péi xù/ - to train

1982. 佩服/pèi fu/ - to admire

1983. 配合/pèi hé/ - to coordinate

1984. 碰见/pèng jiàn/ - to run into

1985. 披/pī/ - to drape over one's shoulder

1986. 批准/pī zhǔn/ - to approve

1987. 飘/piāo/ - to float in the air

1988. 漂/piāo/ - to float on the water

1989. 评价/píng jià/ - to evaluate; to assess

1990. 破产/pò chǎn/ - to go bankrupt

1991. 破坏/pò huài/ - to destroy; destruction; damage

1992. 期待/qī dài/ - to look forward to; expectation

1993. 启发/qǐ fā/ - to enlighten; to inspire

1994. 企图/qǐ tú/ - to attempt

1995. 签/qiān/ - to sign (one's name)
他即将签下一份合同。- He's about to sign another contract.

1996. 签字/qiān zì/ - to sign (one's name); signature
在加入我们之前你需要在此签字。- You need to sign here before joining us.
我认不出这是谁的签字。- I cannot identify this signature.

1997. 欠/qiàn/ - to owe

1998. 强调/qiáng diào/ - to emphasize; to stress

1999. 抢/qiǎng/ - to rob

2000. 瞧/qiáo/ - to see; to look at

2001. 侵略/qīn luè/ - to invade

2002. 勤奋/qín fèn/ - to work hard; diligent
政府必须勤奋工作以重新赢得人民的信任。- The government will have to work hard to win back the confidence of the people.
他勤奋极了。- He is so diligent.

2003. 轻视/qīng shì/ - to despise; contempt

2004. 请求/qǐng qiú/ - to request; request

2005. 庆祝/qìng zhù/ - to celebrate

2006. 娶/qǔ/ - to marry (a woman)

2007. 取消/qǔ xiāo/ - to cancel; cancellation

2008. 去世/qù shì/ - to pass away

2009. 劝/quàn/ - to try to persuade

2010. 缺乏/quē fá/ - to lack; to be short of

2011. 确定/què dìng/ - to confirm; to be sure; to determine
你能确定吗？- Can you confirm this?
你确定锁门了吗？- Are you sure you locked the door?
必须进行检测以确定其对人的长期影响。- Testing must be carried out to determine the long-term effects on humans.

2012. 确认/què rèn/ - to make an identification; to confirm; confirmation

警方正式确认了死者身份。- The police officially confirmed the identity of the deceased.

请书面确认你接受该建议。- Please confirm your acceptance of this offer in writing.

我们在等他们的书面确认。- We're waiting for written confirmation from them.

2013. 燃烧/rán shāo/ - to burn

2014. 热爱/rè ài/ - to adore

2015. 融化/róng huà/ - to melt

2016. 软件/ruǎn jiàn/ - software

2017. 洒/sǎ/ - to sprinkle; to spray

2018. 杀/shā/ - to kill

2019. 晒/shài/ - to dry in the sun; to sunbathe

2020. 删除/shān chú/ - to delete

2021. 善于/shàn yú/ - to be good at

2022. 上当/shàng dàng/ - to be fooled

2023. 舍不得/shě bu de/ - hate to part with; hate to give up or use

我舍不得你。- I hate to part from you.

看着这些菜,我都舍不得动筷子了。- These dishes are so good, I almost don't want to eat them.

2024. 设计/shè jì/ - to design; design

2025. 射击/shè jī/ - to shoot

2026. 生产/shēng chǎn/ - to manufacture; to produce; to give birth (to a child)

我的妻子即将生产。- My wife is about to give birth.

2027. 生长/shēng zhǎng/ - to grow

2028. 省略/shěng lüè/ - to omit; omission

2029. 失业/shī yè/ - to lose one's job

2030. 失去/shí qù/ - to lose

2031. 实践/shí jiàn/ - to put into practice; practices
认识从实践开始。- Knowledge begins with practice.
下一步就是要将理论付诸实践。- The next step is to put the theory into practice.

2032. 实现/shí xiàn/ - to come true; to realize
我的愿望实现了。- My wishes have been realized.
他的梦想实现了。- His dream came true.

2033. 实行/shí xíng/ - to carry out; to implement

2034. 实验/shí yàn/ - to experiment; experiment

2035. 受伤/shòu shāng/ - to be injured; to be wounded

2036. 输入/shū rù/ - to input; input

2037. 属于/shǔ yú/ - to belong to

2038. 摔倒/shuāi dǎo/ - to fall down; to throw someone to the ground

2039. 说服/shuō fú/ - to persuade; to convince

2040. 思考/sī kǎo/ - to think
显然你需要更多的时间来思考。- It's obvious that you need more time to think.

2041. 撕/sī/ - to tear; to rip

2042. 搜索/sōu suǒ/ - to search

2043. 随手/suí shǒu/ - (to do something without extra trouble)
出门请随手关灯。- Please switch off the lights when you leave.

2044. 缩短/suō duǎn/ - to shorten; to cut
吸烟会缩短你的寿命。- Smoking can shorten your life.
一年的课程被缩短为六个月。- The year-long course was cut into six months.

2045. 缩小/suō xiǎo/ - to narrow; to zoom in; to shrink
这是缩小它们之间差距的主要方法。- This is the main way we can close the distance between them.

你可以在流程上进行缩小和放大。- You can zoom in and out on the process.

他的毛衣放到热水里一洗就缩小了。- His sweater shrank when washed in hot water.

2046. 锁/suǒ/ - to lock; lock

2047. 谈判/tán pàn/ - to negotiate; negotiation

2048. 逃/táo/ - to escape; to flee

凶手最终还是逃了。- The killer finally escaped.

他逃进大山里。- He fled into the mountain.

2049. 逃避/táo bì/ - to evade; to avoid; to escape; to run away

她在试图逃避为自己的行为承担全部责任。- She is trying to evade all responsibility for her behavior.

据说有几百人为逃避逮捕而藏了起来。- Hundreds of people are said to have gone into hiding to avoid arrest.

狐狸正在试图逃避猎犬。- The fox is trying to escape from the hound.

你不能永远逃避。- You can't run away forever.

2050. 讨价还价/tǎo jià huán jià/ - to bargain

不要害怕讨价还价。- Don't be afraid to bargain.

2051. 疼爱/téng ài/ - to love dearly

2052. 提倡/tí chàng/ - to advocate

2053. 提问/tí wèn/ - to question

2054. 体会/tǐ huì/ - to get to know something (through learning or by experience)

2055. 体现/tǐ xiàn/ - to embody

2056. 体验/tǐ yàn/ - to experience (for oneself); experience

我需要从教育事业中抽出时间来体验人生。- I needed some time off from school to experience life.

这并不是我所期待的那种平静的体验。- It wasn't the peaceful experience I had expected.

2057. 调整/tiáo zhěng/ - to adjust; adjustment

2058. 挑战/tiǎo zhàn/ - to challenge; challenge
2059. 统一/tǒng yī/ - to unify
2060. 统治/tǒng zhì/ - to rule
2061. 偷/tōu/ - to steal
2062. 投资/tóu zī/ - to invest; investment
2063. 投入/tóu rù/ - to invest in; to put into; to throw into; to be absorbed
一大笔资金投入了各分公司。- A large amount of capital is invested in all these branches.
更经济地节能技术在发达国家已经投入使用。- More cost-effective energy conservation techniques have been put into operation in developed countries.
老实交税，不然的话就与可能被投入监狱。- Pay your taxes honestly, or you may be thrown into jail.
我做事太过投入以致于对周围发生的事毫无反应。- I got so absorbed in doing something that I was unaware of what happened around me.
2064. 吐/tǔ/ - to spit
/tù/ - throw up; to vomit
2065. 推辞/tuī cí/ - to decline (an appointment, invitation, position, etc.)
2066. 推广/tuī guǎng/ - to popularize
2067. 推荐/tuī jiàn/ - to recommend; recommendation
2068. 退/tuì/ - to move back
2069. 退步/tuì bù/ - to regress
2070. 退休/tuì xiū/ - to retire; retirement
2071. 完善/wán shàn/ - to perfect; to improve
他把更多时间用于完善舞蹈动作，而不是健身训练。- He spent more time perfecting his dance moves instead of doing gym work.

外科手术的技术不断得到完善。- Surgical techniques are constantly being improved.

2072. 往返/wǎng fǎn/ - to come and go; to go there and back

2073. 危害/wēi hài/ - to endanger

扩大城市面积危害野生动植物。- The spread of urban areas endangers wildlife.

2074. 威胁/wēi xié/ - to threaten; threat

2075. 违反/wéi fǎn/ - to violate

2076. 维护/wéi hù/ - to maintain; maintenance

2077. 围绕/wéi rào/ - to revolve around

整部电影围绕毒品、性和暴力来展开。- The entire film revolves around drugs, sex and, violence.

2078. 委屈/wěi qu/ - to feel wronged

2079. 委托/wěi tuō/ - to entrust

2080. 问候/wèn hòu/ - to greet

2081. 吸取/xī qǔ/ - to absorb; to draw

你想吸取你需要的知识就得付出时间和努力。- It takes time and effort for one to absorb the knowledge they need.

我们可以从大师们的作品中吸取营养。- We can draw nourishment from the masterpieces.

2082. 吸收/xī shōu/ - to absorb

干沙子易吸水。- Dry sand absorbs water easily.

2083. 下载/xià zǎi/ - to download

2084. 显得/xiǎn de/ - to seem; to look

他显得有点紧张。- He seems a bit nervous.

他显得苍老了。- He looks old.

2085. 显示/xiǎn shì/ - to show; to display

2086. 相处/xiāng chǔ/ - to get along

2087. 相关/xiāng guān/ - to be related to

2088. 想念/xiǎng niàn/ - to miss

2089. 想象/xiǎng xiàng/ - to imagine

2090. 享受/xiǎng shòu/ - to enjoy

2091. 象征/xiàng zhēng/ - to symbolize; to stand for; symbol

2092. 消费/xiāo fèi/ - to consume

2093. 消化/xiāo huà/ - to digest; digestion

2094. 消灭/xiāo miè/ - to annihilate; to eliminate

2095. 消失/xiāo shī/ - to disappear

2096. 销售/xiāo shòu/ - to sell; sale

2097. 歇/xiē/ - to take a rest

让我歇一下。- Please let me take a rest.

2098. 协调/xié tiáo/ - to cohere; to coordinate

装饰物与设计的基调不协调。- The decorations do not cohere with the basic design.

必须协调好城市规划和土地分配之间的关系。- City planning and land allocation has to be coordinated.

2099. 欣赏/xīn shǎng/ - to appreciate

任何人都能欣赏我们的音乐。- Anyone can appreciate our music.

2100. 形成/xíng chéng/ - to form

2101. 形容/xíng róng/ - to describe

2102. 醒/xǐng/ - to wake

2103. 修改/xiū gǎi/ - to amend; to modify

2104. 叙述/xù shù/ - to relate (a story or information)

2105. 宣布/xuān bù/ - to declare; to announce

2106. 宣传/xuān chuán/ - to disseminate

2107. 选举/xuǎn jǔ/ - to elect; election

2108. 询问/xún wèn/ - to inquire

2109. 寻找/xún zhǎo/ - to look for; to seek

2110. 训练/xùn liàn/ - to train; training

2111. 延长/yán cháng/ - to extend; to prolong

2112. 痒/yǎng/ - to itch; itchy

2113. 咬/yǎo/ - to bite

2114. 移动/yí dòng/ - to move; mobile

2115. 移民/yí mín/ - to immigrate; immigration

2116. 遗憾/yí hàn/ - to regret; regret, pity

我遗憾地接受了他的辞职。- I accepted his resignation with regret

我很遗憾地通知你他已因伤势太重不治身亡了。- I regret to inform you that he died as a result of his injuries.

真遗憾！- What a pity!

2117. 一路平安/yí lù píng ān/ - to have a pleasant journey

2118. 议论/yì lùn/ - to talk about

不要在背后议论别人。- Don't talk about others behind their backs.

2119. 印刷/yìn shuā/ - to print; printing

2120. 迎接/yíng jiē/ - to receive (someone)

他到车站迎接客人去了。- He went to the door to greet his visitors.

2121. 营业/yíng yè/ - to open (for business)

超市上午九点开始营业。- The supermarket opens at nine in the morning.

2122. 应付/yìng fu/ - to deal with; to cope with; to make do; perfunctory

我觉得我能应付。- I think I can deal with it.

他能够应付当前的形势。- He can cope with the present situation.

我这个提包还能应付一阵子。- I can make do with this handbag for some time.

对客户采取应付态度是不对的。- It would be wrong to adopt a perfunctory attitude towards clients.

/yīng fù/ - payable

我们下个月会付大额应付账款吗？- Shall we pay the majority of our accounts payable next month?

2123. 应聘/yìng pìn/ - to apply for a position

2124. 应用/yìng yòng/ - to use; to apply; application

这种药应用广泛。- This medicine is widely used.

他的想法是将几何学应用到力学上。- His idea was to apply geometry to dynamics.

我不用退出游戏就可以打开其他应用程序。- I can open other applications without having to exit my game.

拥抱/yōng bào/ - to hug; to embrace; to hold in one's arms; hug

2125. 油炸/yóu zhá/ - to fry

2126. 游览/yóu lǎn/ - to go sightseeing

2127. 犹豫/yóu yù/ - to hesitate

2128. 娱乐/yú lè/ - to amuse; amusement; entertainment

2129. 预订/yù dìng/ - to reserve; reservation

2130. 预防/yù fáng/ - to take precautions against

2131. 运输/yùn shū/ - to transport; transportation

2132. 运用/yùn yòng/ - to apply

这样他们就能更好地把理论运用到实践中去。- In this way, they can better apply theory to practice.

2133. 在乎/zài hu/ - to care about

2134. 赞成/zàn chéng/ - to approve; to agree with

2135. 赞美/zàn měi/ - to eulogize

2136. 造成/zào chéng/ - to cause

2137. 责备/zé bèi/ - to blame

2138. 摘/zhāi/ - to pick (flowers, fruit, etc.); to take off (glasses, hat, etc.)

2139. 粘贴/zhān tiē/ - to paste

2140. 展开/zhǎn kāi/ - to unfold

2141. 涨/zhǎng/ - to rise (of prices, rivers)

2142. 掌握/zhǎng wò/ - to master

2143. 招待/zhāo dài/ - to entertain

我再也不想招待客人了。- I don't want to entertain guests anymore.

2144. 着火/zháo huǒ/ - to catch fire

2145. 着凉/zháo liáng/ - to catch a cold

2146. 召开/zhào kāi/ - to convene (a conference or meeting)

2147. 针对/zhēn duì/ - to be directed against; to be aimed at

该条约不针对任何第三国。- The treaty is not directed against any third country.

这些话不是针对你说的。- These remarks are not aimed at you.

2148. 珍惜/zhēn xī/ - to cherish; to value; to treasure

2149. 诊断/zhěn duàn/ - to diagnose; diagnosis

2150. 振动/zhèn dòng/ - to vibrate; vibration

2151. 睁/zhēng/ - to open (eyes)

2152. 争论/zhēng lùn/ - to argue; to debate; argument

2153. 争取/zhēng qǔ/ - to fight for; to win over

2154. 征求/zhēng qiú/ - to solicit; to request (opinions, feedback, etc.)

2155. 挣钱/zhèng qián/ - to make money

2156. 执行/zhí xíng/ - to carry out; to implement

2157. 指导/zhǐ dǎo/ - to guide; guidance

2158. 指挥/zhǐ huī/ - to command; commander

2159. 制定/zhì dìng/ - to formulate; to draw up

2160. 制作/zhì zuò/ - to make

我用纸和胶水制作了一个模型。- I made a model out of paper and glue.

2161. 治疗/zhì liáo/ - to cure; medical treatment; cure

他的癌症只能控制，无法治疗。- His cancer can only be controlled, not cured.

她正在进行治疗。- She is under medical treatment.

尚没有治疗感冒的特效药。- There is still no cure for a cold.

2162. 煮 /zhǔ/ - to boil

2163. 主持 /zhǔ chí/ - to host

2164. 主动 /zhǔ dòng/ - to take the initiative

2165. 嘱咐 /zhǔ fu/ - to enjoin

2166. 祝福 /zhù fú/ - to wish; blessings

你父亲和我都祝福你。- You father and I wish you well.

我们向您献上新年的祝福。- We offer new year blessings to you.

2167. 注册 /zhù cè/ - to register (a company, website, etc.)

2168. 抓紧 /zhuā jǐn/ - to grasp firmly; to hold on tight

2169. 专心 /zhuān xīn/ - to concentrate; concentration

2170. 转变 /zhuǎn biàn/ - to change

2171. 转告 /zhuǎn gào/ - to pass on (news, messages, information, etc.)

2172. 装饰 /zhuāng shì/ - to decorate; decoration

2173. 追求 /zhuī qiú/ - to pursue

2174. 咨询 /zī xún/ - to consult; consultation

2175. 自豪 /zì háo/ - to be proud of someone or something (in a good way)

2176. 组成 /zǔ chéng/ - to form; to compose

他们组成了一个中文初级班。- They formed a group for beginners in Chinese.

海水主要由水和盐组成。- Seawater is mainly composed of water and salt.

2177. 组合 /zǔ hé/ - to assemble; combination

2178. 阻止 /zǔ zhǐ/ - to prevent

2179. 醉 /zuì/ - to be drunk

2180. 尊敬 /zūn jìng/ - to respect

2181. 遵守/zūn shǒu/ - to comply with; to abide by

2182. 综合/zōng hé/ - to synthesize; comprehensive

你能把这些文件综合成一个吗？- Can you combine these files into one?

学生正在进行全学期功课的综合复习。- The students were doing a comprehensive review of the semester's work.

Chapter 10. Other Content and Function Words (A ~ L)

2183. 暧昧/ài mèi/ - ambiguous

2184. 昂贵/áng guì/ - very expensive

2185. 暗/àn/ - dark; gloomy

2186. 霸道/bà dào/ - overbearing

2187. 薄/báo/ - thin (of thickness)

2188. 宝贵/bǎo guì/ - valuable; precious

2189. 悲观/bēi guān/ - pessimistic

2190. 必然/bì rán/ - inevitable

2191. 必需/bì xū/ - necessary; essential

这些参考书是我们所必需的。- These reference books are necessary to us.

为了帮助提供必需得营养，我们调配了这些营养饮品。- To help provide essential nourishment, we've put together these nutritious drinks.

2192. 必要/bì yào/ - necessary; essential

所有必要条件都满足了。- All the necessary conditions were fulfilled.

我们有必要处理这个棘手的问题。- It is essential that we tackle this thorny problem.

2193. 博大精深/bó dà jīng shēn/ - broad and profound

2194. 不断/bú duàn/ - constant; continuous

2195. 不耐烦/bú nài fán/ - impatience; impatient; impatiently
她做了个不耐烦的动作。- She made a movement of impatience.
要知道我当时已经不耐烦了。- You know, I was getting impatient.
"我都说了我愿意，"他不耐烦地说。- "I told you I did," he replied impatiently.

2196. 不要紧/bú yào jǐn/ - unimportant; nothing serious; it doesn't matter; never mind
这鞋小点不要紧，穿穿就大了。- It doesn't matter if the shoes feel a bit tight, they'll stretch with wear.
不要紧。心意到了就行。- Never mind. It's the thought that counts.
这只是件不要紧的小事。- This is just an unimportant issue.
有点感冒，不要紧。- Just a slight cold, nothing serious

2197. 不像话/bú xiàng huà/ - unreasonable; outrageous

2198. 不安/bù ān/ - unpeaceful; worried; disturbed
听了这消息我心里很不安。- I was rather disturbed by the news.

2199. 不可思议/bù kě sī yì/ - inconceivable

2200. 不相上下/bú xiāng shàng xià/ - to be roughly the same; to be about equal

2201. 不足/bù zú/ - insufficient; not enough; inadequate

2202. 残酷/cán kù/ - cruel

2203. 惭愧/cán kuì/ - ashamed

2204. 残忍/cán rěn/ - ruthless

2205. 苍白/cāng bái/ - pale

2206. 超级/chāo jí/ - super

2207. 潮湿/cháo shī/ - moist; damp
2208. 彻底/chè dǐ/ - thorough; thoroughly
2209. 沉默/chén mò/ - silent
2210. 诚恳/chéng kěn/ - sincere
2211. 持续/chí xù/ - sustainable; to continue
2212. 迟疑/chí yí/ - hesitate
2213. 充分/chōng fèn/ - abundant
2214. 抽象/chōu xiàng/ - abstract
2215. 丑/chǒu/ - ugly
2216. 臭/chòu/ - stink; smelly
2217. 出色/chū sè/ - remarkable
2218. 初级/chū jí/ - primary
2219. 垂直/chuí zhí/ - vertical
2220. 次要/cì yào/ - secondary
2221. 匆忙/cōng máng/ - hasty
2222. 粗糙/cū cāo/ - rough (of surface, feeling, etc.)
2223. 大方/dà fang / - generous
2224. 大型/dà xíng/ - largescale; wide scale; broadscale
2225. 单纯/dān chún/ - innocent; simple; merely

她很单纯。- She's innocent.

她像个孩子一样单纯。- She is as simple as a child.

在生产中不要单纯地追求数量。- Don't merely strive for quantity of production.

2226. 单调/dān diào/ - monotonous
2227. 单独/dān dú/ - by oneself; on one's own; alone
2228. 淡/dàn/ - light (in color); tasteless
2229. 当地/dāng dì/ - local; in the locality
2230. 地道/dì dao/ - pure; typical

她的上海话说得真地道。- She speaks in a pure Shanghai dialect.

他是个地道的美国人。- He is a typical American.
/dì dào/ - tunnel

2231. 独立/dú lì/ - independent; independence

2232. 独特/dú tè/ - unique; distinct

2233. 多余/duō yú/ - superfluous; unnecessary
这么做是多余的。- It is unnecessary to do this.

2234. 恶劣/è liè/ - vile; appalling
天气一直很恶劣。- The weather was consistently vile.
他们已经在恶劣的条件下生活了两个月了。- They have been living in the most appalling conditions for the last two months.

2235. 发达/fā dá/ - developed

2236. 繁荣/fán róng/ - prosperous; booming (economy)

2237. 疯狂/fēng kuáng/ - crazy; madness

2238. 干脆/gān cuì/ - straightforward; clear-cut

2239. 高档/gāo dàng/ - superior quality; top grade

2240. 个人/gè rén/ - individual

2241. 根本/gēn běn/ - fundamental; basic; basis

2242. 公开/gōng kāi/ - public; to make public
没有人对总统公开表示反对。- There's no public demonstration of opposition to the president.
他就队伍的表现公开道歉。- He made a public apology for the team's performance.

2243. 公平/gōng píng/ - fair

2244. 古典/gǔ diǎn/ - classical; classic

2245. 固定/gù dìng/ - static; to stabilize

2246. 乖/guāi/ - well behaved; (of a child or pet) obedient

2247. 光滑/guāng huá/ - smooth; sleek

2248. 光明/guāng míng/ - bright

2249. 广大/guǎng dà/ - vast

2250. 广泛/guǎng fàn/ - extensive; wide range

2251. 豪华/háo huá/ - luxurious

2252. 好客/hào kè/ - hospitality; to treat guests well; hospitable

2253. 好奇/hào qí/ - curious

2254. 合法/hé fǎ/ - lawful; legal

2255. 合理/hé lǐ/ - reasonable

2256. 怀孕/huái yùn/ - pregnant; pregnancy

2257. 慌张/huāng zhāng/ - panic; flurried

2258. 活跃/huó yuè/ - active; vigorous

2259. 基本/jī běn/ - basic; fundamental

2260. 激烈/jī liè/ - intense

2261. 寂寞/jì mò/ - lonely; alone

2262. 坚强/jiān qiáng/ - staunch; strong

她是个坚强而有原则的女人。- She is a strong, principled woman.

2263. 艰巨/jiān jù/ - arduous (task); formidable (project)

任务艰巨，同时时间又很紧迫。- The task is arduous, and there's also not much time.

该工程非常艰巨。- This is a formidable project.

2264. 坚决/jiān jué/ - firmly; resolutely; determined

我坚决不向病毒屈服。- I was determined not to succumb to the virus.

2265. 艰苦/jiān kǔ/ - difficult (of circumstances); hard (of time); arduous (of work); awful (of condition)

艰苦的环境能磨炼人的意志。- Difficult circumstances can temper one's will.

对她而言，那是一段非常艰苦的岁月。- It had been a hard time for her.

我们要耐着性子做艰苦的工作。- We must have patience in doing arduous work.

那里的条件很艰苦。- The conditions there are awful.

2266. 尖锐/jiān ruì/ - keen; sharp; bitter (of criticism)

他看问题很尖锐。- He sees things with a keen eye.

这些话讲得尖锐，但值得考虑。- These remarks are quite sharp, but worth consideration.

他对政府提出了尖锐的批评。- He levied bitter criticism against the government.

2267. 狡猾/jiǎo huá/ - crafty

2268. 结实/jiē shi/ - solid; sturdy; sturdily

这把椅子很结实。- This is a very solid chair.

这孩子又结实又健康。- This child is sturdy and healthy.

这艘船造得结实。- This boat was sturdily made.

2269. 紧/jǐn/ - tight

2270. 紧急/jǐn jí/ - urgent; emergency

2271. 谨慎/jǐn shèn/ - cautious

2272. 经典/jīng diǎn/ - classical; the classics

2273. 敬爱/jìng ài/ - respected

2274. 具体/jù tǐ/ - concrete; specific

2275. 巨大/jù dà/ - gigantic; enormous

2276. 均匀/jūn yún/ - well distributed; uniform

2277. 可见/kě jiàn/ - it can clearly be seen; visible

2278. 可靠/kě kào/ - reliable

2279. 可怕/kě pà/ - fearful; awful; frightful; to be afraid of; terrifying

我刚做了个非常可怕的梦。- I just had the most awful dream.

没有什么可怕的。- There's nothing to be afraid of.

昨晚他再次体验到了那种可怕的折磨。- Last night, he relived his terrifying ordeal.

2280. 客观/kè guān/ - objective

我很想听听你对此事的客观见解。- I would really like to have your objective opinion on this.

2281. 恐怖/kǒng bù/ - horrible; terror

2282. 空闲/kòng xián/ - free (time); idle

2283. 宽/kuān/ - wide; broad; width

2284. 老实/lǎo shi/ - frank

老实跟你讲，我可能犯了个错。- To be frank with you, I may have made a mistake.

2285. 乐观/lè guān/ - optimistic

2286. 立方/lì fāng/ - cubic

2287. 连忙/lián máng/ - promptly

2288. 连续/lián xù/ - continuous

2289. 良好/liáng hǎo/ - good

2290. 了不起/liǎo bu qǐ/ - amazing; great

我最喜欢的书是《了不起的盖茨比》。- *The Great Gatsby* is my favorite book.

2291. 灵活/líng huó/ - flexible

2292. 密切/mì qiè/ - to be close with; closely; intimate

我和她关系密切。- I'm close with her.

轻工业和农业密切相关。- Light industry is closely related to agriculture.

在中世纪，宗教和炼金术密切相联。- Religion had an intimate association with alchemy during the Middle Ages.

2293. 苗条/miáo tiáo/ - slim

2294. 明显/míng xiǎn/ - obvious; distinct

2295. 模糊/mó hu/ - vague; obscure; to blur

我对这意义还很模糊。- The meaning is still obscure to me.

我对第一见面的记忆很模糊。- My memory of that first meeting was vague.

汗水从额头流到了眼睛里，模糊了他的视线。- Sweat ran from his forehead into his eyes, blurring his vision.

2296. 陌生/mò shēng/ - unfamiliar

2297. 难看/nán kàn/ - ugly

2298. 难免/nán miǎn/ - hard to avoid; difficult to escape from
2299. 能干/néng gàn/ - competent
2300. 疲劳/pí láo/ - tired
2301. 片面/piàn miàn/ - unilateral
2302. 平常/píng cháng/ - ordinary; common; usually
2303. 平等/píng děng/ - equal; equality
2304. 平方/píng fāng/ - square (as in square meter)
2305. 平静/píng jìng/ - calm; tranquil
2306. 迫切/pò qiè/ - urgent
2307. 平均/píng jūn/ - on average; average
2308. 朴素/pǔ sù/ - simple
她穿了身朴素的浅灰色套装。- She was wearing a simple light gray suit.
2309. 谦虚/qiān xū/ - modest
2310. 浅/qiǎn/ - shallow; light (of color)
2311. 巧妙/qiǎo miào/ - ingenious
2312. 亲爱/qīn ài/ - dear
2313. 亲切/qīn qiè/ - lovely; friendly
2314. 勤劳/qín láo/ - industrious; hardworking
他是一个勤劳的人。- He is an industrious man.
中国人民勤劳而勇敢。- Chinese people are brave and hardworking.
2315. 清淡/qīng dàn/ - light (of food, not greasy or strongly favored)
2316. 全面/quán miàn/ - comprehensive
2317. 热烈/rè li/ - warm (welcome, applause, etc.)
2318. 热心/rè xīn/ - enthusiastic; warmhearted
2319. 日常/rì cháng/ - daily
2320. 荣幸/róng xìng/ - honor; to be honored

今天很荣幸能参加你们的晚会。- It is a great honor to be with you at this evening party.

承蒙热情接待，不胜荣幸。- I am greatly honored to be given such a warm reception.

2321. 弱/ruò/ - weak

2322. 傻/shǎ/ - silly; foolish

2323. 善良/shàn liáng/ - kindhearted

2324. 深刻/shēn kè/ - profound

2325. 神秘/shén mì/ - mysterious

2326. 生动/shēng dòng/ - vivid; lively

2327. 时髦/shí máo/ - fashionable; fashion

她穿着一件时髦的裙装。- She wears a fashionable dress.

为赶时髦她花了不少钱。- She spent a lot of money to follow fashion trends.

2328. 时尚/shí shàng/ - fashionable; fashion

在阳光充足的地方过冬成了富人的时尚。- It became fashionable for the rich to spend winter in sunny areas.

《时尚》是美国很受欢迎的杂志。- *Fashion* is a very popular magazine in America.

2329. 实用/shí yòng/ - practical

2330. 手工/shǒu gōng/ - handmade; manual

2331. 舒适/shū shì/ - cozy; comfortable

2332. 熟练/shú liàn/ - skilled

我能够熟练操作电脑。- I'm skilled in operating a computer.

2333. 数码/shù mǎ/ - digital

2334. 私人/sī rén/ - private

2335. 所谓/suǒ wèi/ - so-called

2336. 坦率/tǎn shuài/ - frankness; frank; frankly

她似乎不够坦率。- She seemed to be lacking in frankness.

你可以跟我坦率一点。- You can be frank with me.

坦率来说，我不知道。- Frankly, I don't know why.

2337. 淘气/táo qì/ - naughty

2338. 特殊/tè shū/ - special

2339. 特意/tè yì/ - specially

2340. 体贴/tǐ tiē/ - considerate

2341. 天真/tiān zhēn/ - naïve; innocent

2342. 调皮/tiáo pí/ - naughty

2343. 通常/tōng cháng/ - usual; usually

2344. 痛苦/tòng kǔ/ - suffering; painful

2345. 透明/tòu míng/ - transparent

2346. 完美/wán měi/ - perfect; perfectly; perfection

2347. 完整/wán zhěng/ - complete

这是个完整的故事吗？- Is this a complete story?

2348. 唯一/wéi yī/ - only

这是我能够想到的唯一理由。- This is the only explanation I can think of.

2349. 伟大/wěi dà/ - great

他是个伟大的音乐家。- He is a great musician.

2350. 温暖/wēn nuǎn/ - warm

2351. 温柔/wēn róu/ - tender; gentle

2352. 文明/wén míng/ - civilized; civilization

2353. 稳定/wěn dìng/ - steady; stable; stability; to stabilize

2354. 无奈/wú nài/ - have no choice

万般无奈，我只好自己想办法。- I had no choice but to think of a way out by myself.

2355. 无数/wú shù/ - countless

2356. 无所谓/wú suǒ wèi/ - cannot be said to be; not to matter

这些发明无所谓什么实用价值。- These inventions can't be said to have much practical value.

你是输是赢都无所谓。- It doesn't matter if you win or lose.

2357. 无耻/wú chǐ/ – shameless

2358. 无畏/wú wèi/ – fearless

2359. 瞎/xiā/ – blind

2360. 鲜艳/xiān yàn/ – bright-colored

2361. 显然/xiǎn rán/ – obvious; obviously

2362. 相似/xiāng sì/ – similar; alike
我和他的看法相似。– My ideas are similar to his.
他们的性格很相似。– They are much alike in character.

2363. 消极/xiāo jí/ – negative
每个人都有积极和消极的时候。– Everyone has good and bad moments.

2364. 小气/xiǎo qi/ – petty

2365. 孝顺/xiào shùn/ – filial
她很孝顺父母。– She is extremely filial towards her parents.

2366. 形象/xíng xiàng/ – vivid; image
这树立起了一种强有力的公司形象。– This established a strong corporate image.
他用几句形象的话简述了局势。– He sketched the situation in a few vivid words.

2367. 幸运/xìng yùn/ – lucky; fortunate
你真是个幸运儿。– You are a lucky dog.

2368. 雄伟/xióng wěi/ – magnificent (of building, maintain, etc.)

2369. 虚心/xū xīn/ – modest

2370. 迅速/xùn sù/ – rapid

2371. 严肃/yán sù/ – solemn; solemnity

2372. 业余/yè yú/ – amateur

2373. 英俊/yīng jùn/ – handsome

2374. 拥挤/yōng jǐ/ – to be crowded; congestion

2375. 用功/yòng gōng/ – industrious (in one's studies)
她最近十分用工。– She is very industrious lately.

2376. 优惠/yōu huì/ - preferential

中国的投资政策为外国投资者提供了优惠待遇。- China's investment policy provides preferential treatment to foreign investors.

2377. 优美/yōu měi/ - graceful; beautiful

2378. 悠久/yōu jiǔ/ - long (about culture, tradition, history)

2379. 有利/yǒu lì/ - favorable

这些条款对他们公司有利。- These terms were favorable to their company.

2380. 糟糕/zāo gāo/ - terrible; awful

2381. 窄/zhǎi/ - narrow (of space, mind)

2382. 占线/zhàn xiàn/ - busy (phone calling)

2383. 整个/zhěng gè/ - whole; entire

我走遍了整个半岛。- I had walked around the entire peninsula.
整个程序又开始运行了。- The whole process started all over again.

2384. 重/zhòng/ - heavy (of weight)

2385. 重大/zhòng dà/ - significant

2386. 周到/zhōu dào/ - thoughtful; considerate

2387. 主观/zhǔ guān/ - subjective

2388. 紫/zǐ/ - purple

2389. 自动/zì dòng/ - automatic

2390. 自觉/zì jué/ - on one's own initiative

他学习很自觉。- He studies on his own initiative.

2391. 自私/zì sī/ - selfish; selfishness

2392. 自愿/zì yuàn/ - of one's own will; voluntary

他辞去校长一职并非出于自愿。- He did not resign as headmaster of his own volition.
定于下个月开始施行的方案是自愿性质的。- The scheme, due to begin next month, will be voluntary.

2393. 自以为是/zì yǐ wéi shì/ - to be opinionated; to be self-righteous

2394. 真实/zhēn shí/ - real

2395. 彼此/bǐ cǐ/ - each other

2396. 对方/duì fāng/ - the other side

2397. 个别/gè bié/ - just one or two

2398. 其余/qí yú/ - the rest; remaining

2399. 双方/shuāng fāng/ - both parties; both sides

2400. 他们/tā men/ - they (a group of males or mixed genders)

2401. 她们/tā men/ - they (a group of females)

2402. 它们/tā men/ - they (a group of things, animals, plants, etc.)

2403. 册/cè/ - measure word for books

2404. 吨/dūn/ - ton

2405. 幅/fú/ - measure word for paintings

2406. 届/jiè/ - measure word for events, meetings, elections, sporting fixtures, etc.

2407. 颗/kē/ - measure word for small spheres, pearls, corn grains, teeth, satellites, etc

2408. 克/kè/ - gram

2409. 厘米/lí mǐ/ - centimeter

2410. 秒/miǎo/ - second (time unity); in a very short time

2411. 匹/pǐ/ - measure word for horses, cloth, etc.

2412. 片/piàn/ - measure word for slices, tablets, tracts of land or areas of water, etc.

2413. 项/xiàng/ - measure word for principles, items, clauses, etc.; surname Xiang

2414. 毕竟/bì jìng/ - after all; all in all

2415. 不见得/bú jiàn de/ - not necessarily; not likely

他今晚不见得回来。- He's not likely to come tonight.

对于这种事，发火不见得是最有用的或最能被接受的反应。- Anger is not necessarily the most useful or acceptable reaction to such events.

2416. 不得了/bù dé liǎo/ - desperately serious; extremely; terribly
没什么不得了的事。- There's nothing desperately serious.
她听到那坏消息后伤心得不得了。- She was terribly sad when she heard the bad news.
生意好的不得了。- Business is extremely good.

2417. 曾经/céng jīng/ - previously; ever

2418. 迟早/chí zǎo/ - sooner or later

2419. 从前/cóng qián/ - previously; once upon a time

2420. 的确/dí què/ - indeed

2421. 纷纷/fēn fēn/ - one after another; one by one

2422. 赶快/gǎn kuài/ - immediately; at once

2423. 格外/gé wài/ - especially; particularly

2424. 各自/gè zì/ - respectively

2425. 果然/guǒ rán/ - sure enough; as expected

2426. 过分/guò fèn/ - excessively; excessive

2427. 忽然/hū rán/ - suddenly; all of a sudden

2428. 急忙/jí máng/ - hastily

2429. 简直/jiǎn zhí/ - simply; at all
他的中文简直糟透了。- His Chinese is simply terrible.
这玩意儿简直一点用都没有。- This thing is completely useless.

2430. 尽量/jìn liàng/ - as much as possible; to the greatest extent

2431. 绝对/jué duì/ - absolutely; absolute

2432. 居然/jū rán/ - to one's surprise; unexpectedly

2433. 立即/lì jí/ - immediately
我军立即进行了反击。- Our troops immediately returned fire.
立刻/lì kè/ - at once; immediately
立刻到这来！- Come here at once.

我们会立刻送一份报价给你。- We'll send you a quote immediately.

2434. 临时/lín shí/ - temporarily; temporary

2435. 陆续/lù xù/ - successively; one after another

2436. 目前/mù qián/ - currently; at the present time

2437. 偶然/ǒu rán/ - incidentally; occasional; by chance

2438. 强烈/qiáng liè/ - violently

2439. 悄悄/qiāo qiāo/ - stealthily

2440. 亲自/qīn zì/ - personally

2441. 轻易/qīng yì/ - easily; readily

我不轻易交朋友。- I don't readily make friends.

如果你以为你能轻易打败他，那你会后悔的。- If you think you can easily defeat him, you will regret it.

2442. 忍不住/rěn bu zhù/ - cannot help

2443. 如今/rú jīn/ - nowadays

2444. 始终/shǐ zhōng/ - from beginning to end

2445. 事先/shì xiān/ - in advance

2446. 说不定/shuō bu dìng/ - can't say for sure; may

他说不定走了。- He may have left.

我也说不定。- I can't say for sure.

2447. 丝毫/sī háo/ - at all

这丝毫不会影响我的判断。- It doesn't affect my judgment at all.

2448. 随时/suí shí/ - at any time

2449. 同时/tóng shí/ - at the same time; simultaneously

2450. 相当/xiāng dāng/ - equivalent to

2451. 相对/xiāng duì/ - relatively; face to face

湿度相对较低。- The humidity is relatively low.

我们俩相对而坐。- We were sitting face to face.

2452. 幸亏/xìng kuī/ - fortunately; luckily

幸亏在我们动身前雨就停了。- Fortunately, the rain stopped before we set off.

2453. 依然/yī rán/ - as before; still

2454. 再三/zài sān/ - over and over again

2455. 照常/zhào cháng/ - as usual

2456. 逐步/zhú bù/ - step by step

2457. 逐渐/zhú jiàn/ - gradually

2458. 总算/zǒng suàn/ - at last; finally

你总算回来了！- You're finally back!

开了三天车，总算到家了。- After driving for three days, we finally got home.

2459. 最初/zuì chū/ - at the very beginning

2460. 不然/bù rán/ - or else

2461. 不如/bù rú/ - not as good as; it would be better to

2462. 除非/chú fēi/ - only if; unless

2463. 此外/cǐ wài/ - besides; in addition; furthermore

2464. 从此/cóng cǐ/ - from now on; since then

2465. 从而/cóng ér/ - thus; thereby

2466. 多亏/duō kuī/ - thanks to

2467. 反而/fǎn ér/ - instead; on the contrary

2468. 反复/fǎn fù/ - repeatedly; over and over

2469. 反正/fǎn zhèng/ - whatever happens; anyway

2470. 仿佛/fǎng fú/ - as if

2471. 怪不得/guài bu de/ - no wonder

2472. 何必/hé bì/ - there is no need

2473. 何况/hé kuàng/ - much less; let alone

2474. 或许/huò xǔ/ - perhaps; maybe

2475. 假如/jiǎ rú/ - supposing; if

2476. 据说/jù shuō/ - it is said that

2477. 看来/kàn lái/ - it seems; it appears; looks likely

2478. 宁可 /nìng kě/ - would rather

2479. 是否 /shì fǒu/ - whether (or not)

2480. 似的 /shì de/ - as if

他们完全忽略了这些事实，就仿佛不存在似的。- They completely ignore these facts as if they never existed.

2481. 似乎 /sì hū/ - to seem; as if

前途似乎不太乐观。- The future doesn't seem very hopeful.

听起来他们似乎犯下了一个可怕的错误。- It sounds as if they might have made a terrible mistake.

2482. 万一 /wàn yī/ - just in case; what if

为防万一，我还给他买了一份保险。- I bought an insurance for him just in case.

万一你错了呢？- What if you are wrong?

2483. 要不 /yào bu/ - how about

要不我们去吃中餐？- How about having Chinese food?

2484. 一旦 /yí dàn/ - in case (something happens)

2485. 一再 /yí zài/ - again and again

2486. 以及 /yǐ jí/ - as well as

2487. 以来 /yǐ lái/ - since

该党自1964年独立以来一直执政。- The party has been in power since the country's independence in 1964.

2488. 与其 /yǔ qí/ - rather than

与其坐以待毙不如主动出击。- It's better to take the initiative rather than to wait for death.

2489. 至今 /zhì jīn/ - until now

2490. 至于 /zhì yú/ - as for

2491. 自从 /zì cóng/ - since

自从去年至今他都没回过家。- He hasn't been home since last year.

2492. 总共 /zǒng gòng/ - altogether; in total

2493. 总之/zǒng zhī/ - in a word

2494. 作为/zuò wéi/ - as; conduct

作为作家，我对人物塑造感兴趣。- As a writer, I am interested in characterization.

他的作为无可厚非。- His conduct was blameless.

2495. 啊/a/ - modal particle ending sentence, showing affirmation, approval, exclamation, query, or consent; ah

2496. 哎/āi/ - hey! (interjection used to attract attention or to express surprise or disapprobation)

哎！你听见没有？- Hey! Are you listening to me?

你很讨厌哎！- You're annoying!

2497. 唉/āi/ - to sigh; (interjection to express agreement or recognition)

2498. 哎哟/āi yō/ - ouch

2499. 唉/āi/ - to sigh; (interjection to express agreement or recognition)

2500. 吧/ba/ - (modal particle indicating polite suggestion)

我们去公园吧。- Why don't we go to the park?

Conclusion

Congratulations on making it through to the end. This book should have been useful and informative and provided you with a sound grasp of basic Chinese words.

To wrap up, here are some tips and recommendations for further study:

1. Don't learn just ONE word; learn the WHOLE sentence.

Have you noticed that sometimes when you learn just a single word, you can recognize it and even explain the meaning, but you have no clue how to use it? To avoid this situation, you should watch the context and how you can use this word. Although this book has provided some examples for some hard words, you still need to gather as many example sentences as you can. Yes, it will take more time, but the results should be immediately obvious!

2. To remember a new word, just use it.

Sound easy? – It is!

The hardest part is not to forget about using one new word per day.

Set a goal – to learn one new word every day. You can choose a word in the morning or evening, look at how to use it, then find some examples and the context. You can also prepare some phrases which you can use during the day in advance. Then just go out and use it!

Use it at least three times, and then you'll definitely be able to remember it. You also can try to use the same phrase with different people. The most important thing is just to use it as much as you can.

3. Use memory cards.

One of the easiest ways to learn vocabulary that everyone knows, but often forgets, is memory cards. Instead of wasting time in a queue, you can do something useful, such as repeating words. They're very light so you can bring them everywhere. You will never know when you'll have some free time to repeat vocabulary.

4. Learn vocabulary from a specific topic.

For example, you choose the topic of cooking. Write out and learn all the nouns, verbs, adjectives, and phrases that are associated with cooking. After this, open any video, TV drama, or cartoon about cooking. Just listen to it and try to catch the words you've just learned. Hearing a newly learned word will surely make you remember it for a long time.

5. Incorporate surrounding things in your studies.

How many times a day do you look in the mirror? Now imagine that you stuck a sticker with the name of "mirror" in Chinese on it. You'll see this word so often that there is no way not to remember it. Again, it's better to write a simple sentence instead of just a single word.

Finally, it is recommended that you now take the time to review everything in this book again from the beginning. See if you can understand all the sections better the second time around.

Good luck with your language learning journey!

Check out another book by Language Equipped Travelers

www.ingramcontent.com/pod-product-compliance
Lightning Source LLC
Chambersburg PA
CBHW070047230426
43661CB00005B/796